AROUND THE YEAR
WITH EMMET FOX

ALSO BY EMMET FOX

AROUND THE YEAR
WITH EMMET FOX

A Book of Daily Readings

Emmet Fox

HarperSanFrancisco
A Division of HarperCollinsPublishers

HarperOne

Quotations from the Bible in this book are from the King James Version.

AROUND THE YEAR WITH EMMET FOX: *A Book of Daily Readings.* Copyright 1952, 1953, © 1958 by Harper & Brothers. Copyright 1931, 1932, 1933, 1934, 1935, 1937, 1938, 1939, 1940, 1941, 1942, 1943, 1944, 1945, 1946, 1950 by Emmet Fox. All rights reserved. Printed in the United States of America. No part of this book may be used or reproduced in any manner whatsoever without written permission except in the case of brief quotations embodied in critical articles and reviews. For information address HarperCollins Publishers, 10 East 53rd Street, New York, NY 10022.

HarperCollins books may be purchased for educational, business, or sales promotional use. For information please write: Special Markets Department, HarperCollins Publishers, 10 East 53rd Street, New York, NY 10022.

HarperCollins Web site: http://www.harpercollins.com

HarperCollins®, 📖 ®, and HarperOne™ are trademarks of HarperCollins Publishers.

SECOND HARPERCOLLINS PAPERBACK EDITION PUBLISHED IN 1992

Library of Congress Cataloging-in-Publication Data

Fox, Emmet.
    Around the year with Emmet Fox : a book of daily readings / Emmet Fox.
    — 2nd HarperCollins. pbk. ed.
        p. cm.
    Reprint. Previously published: New York : Harper, 1958.
    ISBN: 978-0-06-250408-1
    1. New Thought. 2. Devotional calendars.   I. Title.
    BF639.F67185
    248.4'8998—dc20   91–55079

        08 09 10 11 12 RRD(H) 50 49 48 47 46 45 44 43 42 41

PREFACE

During Emmet Fox's lifetime, when he was speaking week after week to one of the largest audiences ever to gather to hear one man's thoughts on the religious meaning of life, it was not surprising that the mails were heavy with expressions of gratitude from people who felt that he had given significance and satisfaction to the living of their days. Indeed, the most common phrase was, "You made over my life." Nor was it surprising that the publication of his seven books and many pamphlets should bring nationwide response that swelled to world-wide response as some of his books went into translation.

The surprising thing, even to his publishers who knew something of the extent and depth of his influence, is that seven years after his passing the response continues. Lives are still being changed by the impact of his books. And the impact appears to be the personal sort that is always most arresting, most overwhelming, most rewarding: one individual finds his own attitudes completely transformed and forthwith shares the source of his strength with some other who is in despair, frustration, or sorrow.

Hence the idea was born that a book of daily devotions for his friends and followers might be made from Emmet Fox's unpublished lecture notes and manuscripts. But in order to give the full message of the Gospel as Dr. Fox himself would have wished, an editorial decision was made to lift from both his published and unpublished works the essence of his message. Poetry meant much to Dr. Fox; thus, readings for three days carry only a favorite poem and appropriate Scripture.

In this volume will be found not only these hitherto unpublished directions for daily living but also passages beloved by those who have worn thin a first edition of *The Sermon on the Mount*, say, or *Power Through Constructive Thinking*. But this book in no way takes the place of those fuller discussions of transforming themes, and it is hoped that the abbreviated messages presented here will lead the reader to the older books.

The Sermon on the Mount is now pushing the million-copy-circulation that its author envisioned, and it may go far beyond that number with the increasing need for a handbook of spiritual development that is both inspirational and demanding of personal dedication. The day-by-day perusal of this new volume should bring to life Emmet Fox's words—and, as he would have preferred, the Word.

—The Publishers

There exists a mystic Power that is able to transform your life so thoroughly, so radically, so completely, that when the process is completed your own friends would hardly recognize you, and, in fact, you would scarcely be able to recognize yourself.

It can lift you out of an invalid's bed, and free you to go out into the world to shape your life as you will. It can throw open the prison door and liberate the captive.

This Power can do for you that which is probably the most important thing of all in your present stage: it can find your true place in life for you, and put you into it.

This Power is really no less than the primal Power of Being, and to discover that Power is the divine birthright of all men.

. . . *the kingdom of God is within you* (Luke 17:21).

. . . *seek ye first the kingdom of God . . . and all these things shall be added . . .* (Matthew 6:33).

But where is this wonderful Power to be contacted? The answer is simple—this Power is to be found within your own consciousness, the last place that most people would look for it. Within your own mentality there lies a source of energy stronger than electricity, more potent than high explosive; unlimited and inexhaustible. You only need to make conscious contact with it to set it working in your affairs. This Indwelling Power, the Inner Light, is spoken of in the Bible as a child. The conscious discovery by you that you have this Power within you, and your determination to make use of it, is the birth of the child.

For unto us a child is born, unto us a son is given: and the government shall be upon his shoulder: and his name shall be called Wonderful, Counselor, The Mighty God, The Everlasting Father, The Prince of Peace (Isaiah 9:6).

This is a marvelous description of what happens when the spiritual idea, the Child, is born to the soul. Walking in darkness, moral or physical, dwelling in the land of the shadow of death—the death of joy, or hope, or even self-respect—describes well the condition of many people before this light shines into their weary, heartbroken lives; and the Prophet rises into a paean of exultant joy as he contemplates the deliverance.

The people that walked in darkness have seen a great light: they that dwell in the land of the shadow of death, upon them hath the light shined (Isaiah 9:2).

Once you have contacted the Power within, and have allowed it to take over your responsibilities for you, it will direct and govern all your affairs from the greatest to the least without mistakes. *The government shall be upon his shoulder.* You are tired, and driven, and worried, and weak, and ill, and depressed, because you have been trying to carry the government upon your own shoulder; the burden is too much for you, and you have broken down under it. Now, immediately you hand over your self-government, that is, the burden of making a living, or of healing your body, or erasing your mistakes, to the Child. He, the Tireless One, the All-Powerful, the All-Wise, the All-Resourceful, assumes it with joy; and your difficulties have seen the beginning of the end.

Cast thy burden upon the Lord, and he shall sustain thee . . . (Psalm 55:22).

The prophet Isaiah speaks of the "Name" of the Child, and if we know something of Bible symbolism, we know that we are now going to learn something fundamental, for in the Bible, the *name* of anything means the character or nature of that thing. A name is not merely an arbitrary label, but actually a hieroglyph of the soul. We are given no less than five names or qualities of the Child.

First Isaiah says that the name of the Child is Wonderful. The word *wonderful* used here requires careful scrutinization. As employed in the Bible, it implies a miracle—just that, and nothing less. The Bible repeatedly says that miracles can happen, and it gives detailed and circumstantial accounts of many specific cases. Moreover, it says that miracles always will happen if you believe them to be possible, and are willing to recognize the power of God, and to call upon it.

As soon as the Child is born in your consciousness, the miracle will come into your life. This does not mean simply that you will become resigned to your present circumstances, or that you will then be enabled to meet the same difficulties with a higher courage or a clearer brain. It means the *miracle*.

But Jesus beheld them, and said unto them, With men this is impossible; but with God all things are possible (Matthew 19:26).

4

The prophet Isaiah also calls this Child "Counselor." A counselor is one who gives guidance. If you are worried because you do not know whether to take some important step, to accept a business offer, to sign an important document, to enter upon a partnership, to resign your position, to trust someone, to say something, the Child will be your Counselor.

In the third place the prophet reveals to us who the Child really is. It is no less than God Himself, "The Mighty God." And truly the mystic Power that transforms, and transmutes, and transfigures, is God Himself, always present with you, and always available.

. . . *the Father that dwelleth in me, he doeth the works* (John 14:10). Read John 14:10–17.

The fourth name the prophet Isaiah speaks of is that of Everlasting Father. As Jesus so clearly pointed out, God is our Father, not merely our Creator. But we have to establish our own consciousness of this fact.

In the fifth place, we receive what is perhaps the greatest name of all, "The Prince of Peace." Think what perfect peace of soul, if you could attain it, would actually mean to you. If you had real peace of soul, do you suppose that your body could be ill? Given real peace of soul, how easy it would be to find your true place in the world. How quickly and efficiently you could perform your work. Once you have attained true peace of soul, you have made it possible for the Child to teach you new things, utterly beyond the compass of your present understanding.

Of the increase of his government and peace there shall be no end, upon the throne of David, and upon his kingdom, to order it, and to establish it with judgment and with justice from henceforth even for ever (Isaiah 9:7).

In view of the fact that the weaker souls, the fearful, and the unbelieving, and the depressed, should find it impossible to believe that such good tidings could be true, the prophet clinches the matter with the definite assertion:

. . . The zeal of the Lord of hosts will perform this (Isaiah 9:7).

A great deal of confusion seems to exist in many minds concerning the precise avenue through which realization and harmony are to be attained.

The only solution is to contact the divine Power that dwells within your own soul; and to bring it to bear upon the various difficulties in your life, taking them in due order, that is, attacking the most urgent first. The real remedy for every one of your difficulties is, as we are told on every page of the Bible, to find and *know* the Indwelling Presence.

Acquaint now thyself with him, and be at peace: thereby good shall come unto thee (Job 22:21).

This, then, is the task, and the only one—to find, and consciously know, your own Indwelling Lord. You see now how the confusion disappears, and the perfect simplicity of the whole thing emerges once you realize this fact.

The first step that the earnest student must take to locate the Inner Light within himself is to settle on a definite method of working, selecting whichever one seems to suit him best, and then giving it a fair trial. Merely reading books, making good resolutions, or talking plausibly about the thing will get him nowhere.

Get a definite method of working, practice it conscientiously every day; and stick to one method long enough to give it a fair chance. You would not expect to play the violin after two or three attempts, or to drive a car without a little preliminary practice.

Get to work on some concrete problem, choosing preferably whatever it is that you are most afraid of. Work at it steadily; and if no improvement at all shows itself within, say, a couple of weeks, then try your method on another problem. If you still get no result, then scrap that method and adopt a new one. Remember, there is a way out. The problem really is, not the getting rid of your difficulties, but finding your own best method for doing it.

. . . *Whatsoever ye shall ask the Father in my name, he will give it you* (John 16:23).

There is only one way to make spiritual progress, and that is to practice the Presence of God. Mankind is continually seeking to discover a shortcut but as usual the lazy man takes the most pains in the long run, and having wasted his time in wandering up bypaths, he is ultimately driven by failure and suffering to the realization of the grand truth that there is no substitute for prayer; that is, the conscious dwelling upon the Being of God.

If your intuitive nature is well developed, you will seldom need to use formal statements at all. This is excellent—for who will trouble to climb a ladder when he is strong enough to leap over the wall?

But it must not be overlooked that very many people do all their work with formal statements of Truth, and get consistently good results by working in this way. Not through repeating affirmations like a parrot. Those who work like a parrot inevitably make the parrot's demonstration—they remain in the cage. Of a good worker who used the same phrases many times it was said by a friend: "He constantly uses the old affirmations, but he stuffs them with fresh feeling every time."

The Lord is nigh unto all them that call upon him, to all that call upon him in truth (Psalm 145:18).

Prayer is the one thing that can make a change in your life. If you will go direct to God in simple, affirmative prayer, you can heal your body, bring peace and harmony into your life, and make well-being a reality.

Sometimes discouragement sets in when the answer does not come immediately but God is working on the unseen plane and our part is to be persistent. Persistence in prayer is an expression of our faith, for by our persistence we are affirming our belief that God will make his answer plain.

. . . *men ought always to pray, and not to faint* (Luke 18:1).

Have you ever asked yourself the question: What is God like? We are told to pray by turning away from the problem and thinking about God; but how are we to think about God? What is His nature? What is His character? Where is He? Can we really contact Him, and if so, how?

The first and most fundamental thing to realize is that God is not just a superior kind of man. The Bible says that God is spirit and that they that worship Him must worship Him in spirit and in truth. To worship Him in spirit means to get a spiritual understanding of His nature. To define God would be to limit Him, but we can get an excellent working knowledge of God by considering different aspects of His nature. Of these there are seven main aspects more important than any of the others. These are seven fundamental truths about God, truths that never change. Thinking of any aspect of God will solve a problem in time, but if you select the right aspect you will get your result more quickly and more easily.

For the invisible things of him from the creation of the world are clearly seen, being understood by the things that are made, even his eternal power and Godhead . . . (Romans 1:20).

The first main aspect of God is Life. God is not just living, nor does God give life, but God is Life. Where God is, there Life is.

When you are sick you are only partly alive. When you are tired or depressed or discouraged, you are only partly alive. Few people express God in an adequate way because they lack the sense of life.

Joy is one of the highest expressions of God as Life. Actually it is a mixture of Life and Love, and the Bible says "the sons of God shout for joy." When we realize our divine sonship, we must experience joy. Joy always has an expansive effect, just as fear has a contracting effect. When a person says "I can," you notice an expansive and forward movement, but when he says "I can't," there is a retraction. You could not imagine a person saying, "Yes, I can," with a shrinking gesture, or "No, I can't," in an optimistic or forthright way. The body always expresses the thought; the thought of Life heals and inspires, whereas thoughts of fear and death contract and destroy.

Realizing divine Life heals the sick. Animals usually respond quickly, and plants very quickly indeed, because they do not have that strong sense of personal egotism that most human beings do. They never make up their minds that they cannot get well or that "sickness is sent for a good purpose." Neither do they give way to discouragement because they have not been healed faster.

For God giveth to a man that is good in his sight wisdom and knowledge, and joy . . . (Ecclesiastes 2:26).

The second main aspect of God is Truth. God is not truthful but Truth itself, and wherever there is Truth, there is God. There are many things that are relatively true at certain times and places only, but God is absolute Truth at all times and in all circumstances. As soon as we touch God, who is the Absolute, relative things disappear.

To know the truth about any condition heals it. Jesus said, *And ye shall know the truth, and the truth shall make you free* (John 8:32).

You should realize God as Truth when you want information on any subject, or if you suspect that you have to deal with deceit. If you believe that someone is trying to deceive you, claim that divine Truth dwells in the person concerned, and is expressed through him. If you realize this clearly enough he will then speak the truth. When you have to transact any important business such as signing a lease or a contract, spend a few minutes realizing divine Truth and if there is anything you should know it will come out. Of course people may have no desire to deceive you and yet for some reason you may not be given the whole story. I know of several cases where serious misunderstandings were prevented because somebody realized God as truth and so all the facts were brought out. I know also of cases where intentional dishonesty was frustrated in the same way.

The third main aspect of God is Love. God is not loving but Love itself, and it would probably be true to say that of all of the seven main aspects this is the most important one for us to practice. There is no condition that enough Love will not heal. The Bible deals with the nature of God, and as the Scripture develops, the idea of God becomes clearer until toward the end it says,

. . . *God is love; and he that dwelleth in love dwelleth in God, and God in him* (1 John 4:16).

By this shall all men know that ye are my disciples, if ye have love one to another (John 13:35).

Where there is fear there cannot be love. The best way to rid yourself of fear is to realize divine Love. If you love God more than you love your microbe, your sickness, your grievance, your lack, or your fear, you will be healed. We have all heard many stories of exceptional people who were able to go among wild beasts in the jungle without being hurt, and there are many other histories on record of people who passed through extraordinary dangers of other kinds quite unscathed. To realize God as Love is the remedy for fear.

Divine Love *never* fails, but the important thing to realize is that divine Love must be in your own heart and cannot operate from outside, so to speak. When your prayers are not answered it must be because you have not fulfilled the conditions of the law, and, ninety-nine times in a hundred, it is because you are lacking in a sense of love for all. Practice love every day and watch your thought, and watch your tongue, and watch your deed, that nothing contrary to love finds expression there.

The fourth main aspect of God is Intelligence. When you clearly realize that this is an intelligent universe it will make a major difference in your life. In an intelligent universe there cannot be disharmony because all ideas must work together for the common good. Neither can there be any lack. An engine that has been intelligently designed does not have any unnecessary parts and neither are any essential parts lacking.

It is especially important to realize that God is Intelligence because it sometimes happens that when people outgrow the childish idea that God is just a magnified man, they go to the opposite extreme and think of God as a blind force, like gravity or electricity. This means that they have lost all sense of the Love and Fatherhood of God, and such an idea is very little better than a subtle form of atheism.

God is not a person in the usual sense of the word, but God has every quality of personality except its limitation. The human mind cannot imagine personality that is not limited, but this difficulty arises from the limitation of the human mind itself, and of course this does not affect the nature of God. The Bible says, in effect, whatever you think I am, that will I be to you; this means that if we attribute to God every quality of an infinite, intelligent, loving personality, God will be just that to us. So we may say that we believe in a personal God.

Children and young people respond very readily indeed to a prayer for expression of Intelligence through them. If you are interested in a young person at college, pray several times a week that Intelligence will manifest through him and you will be surprised to find how his progress in his studies will increase. Remember also the wonderful fact that when you work for a person the result will be with him for the rest of his life.

O the depth of the riches both of the wisdom and knowledge of God! . . . (Romans 11:33).

The fifth main aspect of God is Soul. Soul is that aspect of God by virtue of which He is able to individualize Himself. The word *individual* means "undivided." Most people seem to think it suggests separateness but actually individual means undivided, and God has the power of individualizing Himself without, so to speak, breaking Himself into parts.

You are really an individualization of God. Only God can individualize Himself in an infinite number of units of consciousness, and yet not be in any way separate because God is spirit. Matter cannot be individualized. It can only be divided. So your real self, the Christ within, the spiritual man, the I Am, or the divine spark, as it is variously called, is an individualization of God. You are the presence of God at the point where you are.

Man may very well be compared to an electric light bulb. The electric current is present in all parts of the circuit, but it shines forth, or one might say, figuratively, becomes self-conscious, in the bulb. So divine Mind becomes self-conscious in you.

Jesus answered them, Is it not written in your law, I said, Ye are gods? (John 10:34).

When you are called upon to perform some task or undertake some responsibility that seems too great for you, realize that you are one with God and the task will become "*our* business" instead of "*my* business."

The sixth main aspect of God is Spirit. We know that God is Spirit but what does that mean? Spirit is that which cannot be destroyed or damaged. It is the opposite of matter. Matter wears out, but Spirit does not because Spirit is *substance*. Herbert Spencer defines substance as that which is not subject to discord or decay. Webster says, "that which underlies all outward manifestation . . . real, unchanging essence or nature . . . that in which qualities inhere . . . that which constitutes anything that is." All this can only apply to spiritual things.

God is a Spirit: and they that worship him must worship him in spirit and in truth (John 4:24).

You are Spirit. Spirit cannot die and was never born. Your true self was never born and will never die. You are eternal, divine, unchanging Spirit, in your true nature. The whole universe is a spiritual creation but we see it in a limited way. You have sometimes seen a window made of fluted glass, and you know that if you look at the street through this window everything will be distorted. Nevertheless, you know that the distortion arises from your seeing wrongly. Our false vision causes us to know ourselves only from a seeming birth to a seeming death; but this is illusion too. This distorted vision of Spirit is really what we know as "matter." Eucken says, "Reality is an independent spiritual world, unconditioned by the apparent world of sense"—and this is substance.

The seventh main aspect of God is Principle, and this is probably the one that is least understood. What does the word *principle* mean?

Consider a few generally accepted principles. "Water seeks its own level." This is a principle. It is not only the course taken by a particular drop of water in a particular locality. It is true of all water everywhere. "The angles of any triangle always add up to 180 degrees." It makes no matter what kind of triangle one may consider; as long as it is a triangle, this principle holds. These principles were true a billion years ago and they will be true a billion years hence.

Jesus Christ the same yesterday, and today, and for ever (Hebrews 13:8).

Prayer is answered because God is principle, eternally manifest in the same way. When we pray rightly we bring ourselves into harmony with His Law of Being. Prayer does not ask God to change the laws for our temporary convenience, but it tunes us in, so to speak, with divine Principle; if God were to make exceptions because we were in great difficulties (which, because of His nature, He could never do) we should never know where we stood. If the law of gravity were occasionally suspended without notice, say, because a very important man had fallen off a roof, you know what would happen to the world.

Each of the seven main aspects is a distinct quality like the elements in chemistry. A chemical element, as you know, is just itself and nothing else. Oxygen is an element because there is nothing in it but oxygen. Water on the other hand is a compound, a combination of hydrogen and oxygen. There are many attributes of God, such as wisdom, beauty, joy, and so forth, but they are compounds, made up of two or more of the seven main aspects. Wisdom, for example, is the perfect balance of Intelligence and Love.

Beauty is the perfect balance of Life, Truth, and Love. In any true work of art, you will find that these three aspects are balanced. There are many such relationships and interdependencies—"Thou canst not pluck a flower without the trembling of a star."

Study and research are well in their own time and place, but no amount of either will get you out of a concrete difficulty. Nothing but practical work in your own consciousness will do that.

Scientific prayer is the Golden Key to harmony and happiness. You need take no one's word for it, and you should not. Simply try it for yourself, and see.

Whoever you are, wherever you may be, the Golden Key to harmony is in your hand now. This is because it is God who works, and not you, and so your particular limitations or weaknesses are of no account in the process. You are only the channel through which the divine action takes place, and your part is first to get yourself out of the way.

The actual method of working is simplicity itself. All that you have to do is this: *Stop thinking about the difficulty, whatever it is, and think about God instead.* This is the complete rule, and if only you will do this, the trouble, whatever it is, will presently disappear. It may be big or little, it may concern health, finance, a lawsuit, a quarrel, an accident, or anything else conceivable; but whatever it is, just stop thinking about it, and think of God instead—that is all you have to do.

The thing could not be simpler, could it? And yet it never fails to work when given a fair trial.

. . . *with God all things are possible* (Matthew 19:26).

Work by rehearsing everything that you know about God. God is Wisdom, Truth, inconceivable Love. God is present everywhere; has infinite power; knows everything. It matters not how well you may think you understand these things; go over them repeatedly.

The rule is to think about God, and if you are thinking about your difficulty you are not thinking about God. To be continually glancing over your shoulder in order to see how matters are progressing is fatal, because that is thinking of the trouble, and you must think of God, and of nothing else. Your object is to drive the thought of the difficulty right out of your consciousness, for a few moments at least, substituting for it the thought of God. If you can become so absorbed in this consideration of the spiritual world that you really forget for a while all about the trouble concerning which you began to pray, you will presently find that your trouble falls into new perspective, new relationships, so that it is no longer a difficulty.

. . . thou hast made heaven, the heaven of heavens, with all their host, the earth, and all things that are therein, the seas, and all that is therein, and thou preservest them all . . . (Nehemiah 9:6).

Doth not he see my ways, and count all my steps? (Job 31:4).

In order to "Golden Key" a troublesome person or a difficult situation, think, "Now I am going to 'Golden Key' John, or Mary, or that threatened danger"; then lift John or Mary or the danger into the presence of God and think only of God.

Thereafter the person is certain to be in some degree a better, wiser, and more spiritual person. A pending lawsuit or other difficulty will probably fade out without coming to a crisis, justice being done to all parties concerned.

. . . *O Lord God, thou art that God, and thy words be true, and thou hast promised this goodness unto thy servant* (2 Samuel 7:28).

We have said that the Golden Key is simple, and so it is, but, of course, it is not always easy to turn. If you are very frightened or worried it may be difficult, at first, to get your thoughts away from material things. But by constantly repeating some statement of absolute Truth that appeals to you, such as *There is no power but God*, or *I am the child of God, filled and surrounded by the perfect peace of God*, or *God is Love*, or *God is guiding me now*, or, perhaps best and simplest of all, just *God is with me*—you will soon find that your mind is clearing. Do not struggle, be quiet but insistent. Each time that you find your attention wandering, just switch it straight back to God.

Do not try to think out in advance what the solution of your difficulty will probably turn out to be. This is technically called *outlining*, and will only delay the demonstration. Leave the question of ways and means to God. You want to get out of your difficulty—that is sufficient. You do your half, and God will never fail to do His.

. . . *whosoever shall call on the name of the Lord shall be delivered* . . . (Joel 2:32).

There are a few great laws that govern all thinking, just as there are a few fundamental laws in chemistry. We know that thought control is the key of destiny, and in order to learn thought control we have to know and understand these laws.

One of the great mental laws is the Law of *Substitution*. This means that the only way to get rid of a certain thought is to substitute another one for it. You cannot dismiss a thought directly. You can do so only by substituting another one for it. If I say to you, "Do not think of the Statue of Liberty," of course, you immediately think of it. If you say, "I am not going to think of the Statue of Liberty," that is thinking about it. But if you become interested in something else, you forget all about the Statue of Liberty—and this is a case of substitution.

When negative thoughts come to you, do not fight them, but think of something positive. Preferably think of God; but if that is difficult at the moment, turn your attention to something quite different.

But I say unto you, That ye resist not evil . . . (Matthew 5:39).

With him is wisdom and strength, he hath counsel and understanding (Job 12:13).

Another of the great mental laws is the Law of *Relaxation*. In all mental working effort defeats itself. This is just the opposite of what we find on the physical plane, but it will not surprise us because we know that in many cases the laws of mind are the reverse of the laws of matter.

On the physical plane, the harder you press a drill the faster will it go through a plank. The harder you hammer a nail the sooner does it go into the wall. But any attempt at mental pressure is foredoomed to failure because the moment tension begins, the mind stops working creatively. When you try to force things mentally, when you try to hurry mentally, you simply stop your creative power.

In all mental working be relaxed, gentle, and unhurried *for effort defeats itself*.

   . . . *in quietness and in confidence shall be your strength* . . . (Isaiah 30:15).

As soon as the subconscious mind accepts any idea, it immediately begins trying to put it into effect. It uses all its resources (and these are far greater than is commonly supposed) to that end. It uses every bit of knowledge that you have ever collected, most of which you have totally forgotten, to bring about its purpose. It mobilizes the many mental powers that you possess, most of which you never consciously use. It draws on the unlimited energy of the race mind. It lines up all the laws of nature as they operate both inside and outside of you, to get its way.

Sometimes it succeeds in its purpose immediately. Sometimes it takes a little time, sometimes it takes a long time; but if the thing is not utterly impossible, the subconscious will bring it about—*once it accepts the idea.*

This law is true for both good and bad ideas. This law, when used negatively, brings sickness, trouble, and failure; and when used positively, brings healing, freedom, and success. We give the orders—the subconscious does the work.

. . . *his secret is with the righteous* (Proverbs 3:32).

Practice makes perfect. This familiar proverb embodies one of the great laws of human nature and—being a law—it is never under any circumstances broken.

There is simply no achievement without practice and the more practice, provided it is done intelligently, the greater will the proficiency be and the sooner will it be attained. It is true in every conceivable branch of human endeavor. Practice is the price of proficiency.

In metaphysics the effects of this law are particularly striking. Thought control is entirely a matter of intelligent practice. And true religion may well be summed up as the Practice of the Presence of God.

    . . . *be ye doers of the word, and not hearers only* . . . (James 1:22).

It is an unbreakable mental law that you have to forgive others if you want to demonstrate over your difficulties and to make any real spiritual progress.

The vital importance of forgiveness may not be obvious at first sight, but you may be sure that it is not by chance that every great spiritual teacher from Jesus Christ downward has insisted so strongly upon it.

You must forgive injuries, not just in words, or as a matter of form, but in your heart—and that is the long and the short of it. You do this, not for the other person's sake, but for your own sake. Resentment, condemnation, anger, desire to see someone punished are things that rot your soul. Such things fasten your troubles to you with rivets. They fetter you to many other problems that actually have nothing whatever to do with the original grievances themselves.

Not rendering evil for evil, or railing for railing: but contrariwise blessing; knowing that ye are thereunto called, that ye should inherit a blessing (1 Peter 3:9).

Every thought is made up of two factors, knowledge and feeling. A thought consists of a piece of knowledge with a charge of feeling, and it is the feeling alone that gives power to the thought. No matter how important or magnificent the knowledge content may be, if there is no feeling attached to it nothing will happen. On the other hand, no matter how unimportant or insignificant the knowledge content may be, if there is a large charge of feeling something will happen.

It makes no difference whether the knowledge content is correct or not as long as you believe it to be correct. Remember that it is what we really believe that matters. A report about something may be quite untrue, but if you believe it, it has the same effect upon you as if it were true; and that effect again will depend upon the quantity of feeling attached to it.

When we understand this law we see the importance of accepting the truth with joy in every phase of our experience.

Thou wilt show me the path of life: in thy presence is fullness of joy . . . (Psalm 16:11).

What you think upon grows. This is an Eastern maxim, and it sums up neatly the greatest and most fundamental of all the laws of mind.

What you think upon grows. Whatever you allow to occupy your mind you magnify in your own life. Whether the subject of your thought be good or bad, the law works and the condition grows. Any subject that you keep out of your mind tends to diminish in your life, because what you do not use atrophies.

The more you think about your grievances or the injustices that you have suffered, the more such trials will you continue to receive; the more you think of the good fortune you have had, the more good fortune will come to you.

This is the basic, fundamental, all-inclusive law of mind, and actually all psychological and metaphysical teaching is little more than commentary upon this.

What you think upon grows.

Finally, brethren, whatsoever things are true, whatsoever things are honest, whatsoever things are just, whatsoever things are pure, whatsoever things are lovely, whatsoever things are of good report; if there be any virtue, and if there be any praise, think on these things (Philippians 4:8).

Truth is within ourselves; it takes no rise
From outward things, whate'er you may believe.
There is an inmost centre in us all,
Where truth abides in fullness; and around,
Wall upon wall, the gross flesh hems it in,
This perfect, clear perception—which is truth.

A baffling and perverting carnal mesh
Binds it, and makes all error: and to *know*,
Rather consists in opening out a way
Whence the imprisoned splendour may escape,
Than in effecting entry for a light
Supposed to be without.
　　　　—Robert Browning, "Paracelsus." Part I

. . . ye shall know the truth, and the truth shall make you free (John 8:32).

The Lord's Prayer is the most important of all the Christian documents. Everyone who is seeking to follow along the Way that Jesus led, should pray the Lord's Prayer intelligently every day.

The Great Prayer is a compact formula for the development of the soul. It is designed with the utmost care for that specific purpose; so that those who use it regularly, with understanding, will experience a real change of soul. It is the change of soul that matters. The mere acquisition of knowledge received intellectually makes no change in the soul.

The first thing that we notice is that the prayer naturally falls into seven clauses. This is very characteristic of the Oriental tradition. Seven symbolizes individual completeness, the perfection of the individual soul, just as the number twelve in the same convention stands for corporate completeness. The seven clauses are put together in perfect order and sequence, and they contain everything that is necessary for the nourishment of the soul. The more one analyzes the Lord's Prayer, the more wonderful its construction is seen to be.

After this manner therefore pray ye . . . (Matthew 6:9).

This simple statement fixes clearly the nature and character of God. It tells all that man needs to know about God, and about himself, and about his neighbor. Oliver Wendell Holmes said: "My religion is summed up in the first two words of the Lord's Prayer."

"Our Father." In this clause Jesus lays down once and for all that the relationship between God and man is that of father and child. This eliminates any possibility that the Deity could be the relentless and cruel tyrant. The majority of men and women are at their best in dealing with their children. Speaking of the same truth elsewhere, Jesus said:

If ye then, being evil, know how to give good gifts unto your children, how much more shall your Father which is in heaven give good things to them that ask him? (Matthew 7:11).

Note that this clause that fixes the nature of God, at the same time fixes the nature of man. It is a cosmic law that like begets like. It is not possible that a rosebush should produce lilies, or that a cow should give birth to a colt. The offspring must be of the same nature as the parent; and so, since God is divine Spirit, man must essentially be divine Spirit too, whatever appearances may say to the contrary.

At a single blow this teaching of Jesus swept away 99 percent of all the old theology, with its avenging God, its chosen and favored individuals, its eternal hell fire, and all the other horrible paraphernalia of man's diseased and terrified imagination. God exists—and the Eternal, All-Powerful, All-Present God is the loving Father of mankind.

If you would meditate upon this fact, until you had some degree of understanding of what it really means, most of your difficulties and physical ailments would disappear, for they are rooted in fear. If only you could realize to some extent that Omnipotent Wisdom is your living, loving Father, most of your fears would go. If you could realize it completely, every negative thing in your life would vanish away. Now you see the object that Jesus had in mind when he placed this clause first.

So God created man in his own image, in the image of God created he him (Genesis 1:27).

Now the Prayer says, not "My Father," but "Our Father," and this indicates beyond the possibility of mistake, the truth of the brotherhood of man. It forces upon our attention at the very beginning the fact that all men are the children of one Father; and that

There is neither Jew nor Greek, there is neither bond nor free, there is neither male nor female: for ye are all one in Christ Jesus (Galatians 3:28).

Here Jesus cuts away the illusion that the members of any nation, or race, or territory, or group, or class, or color, are, in the sight of God, superior to any other group.

The final point is the implied command that we are to pray not only for ourselves but for all mankind. None of us lives to himself, however we may try. In a much more literal sense than people are aware we are limbs of one Body.

"Our Father"—a spiritual explosive, that will ultimately destroy every kind of human bondage.

He prayeth well, who loveth well
Both man and bird and beast;
He prayeth best, who loveth best
All things both great and small:
For the dear God who loveth us,
He made and loveth all.
                              —Coleridge

But ask now the beasts, and they shall teach thee; and the fowls of the air, and they shall tell thee: Or speak to the earth, and it shall teach thee: and the Fishes of the sea shall declare unto thee . . . that the hand of the Lord hath wrought this (Job 12:7–9).

Having clearly established the Fatherhood of God and the brotherhood of man, Jesus next goes on to describe the fundamental facts of existence. It is the nature of God to be in heaven, and of man to be on earth because God is Cause, and man is manifestation. Here *heaven* stands for God or Cause, because in religious phraseology heaven is the term for the Presence of God. The word *earth* signifies manifestation, and man's function is to manifest or express God as Cause. In other words, God is the Infinite and Perfect Cause of all things; but Cause has to be expressed, and God expresses Himself by means of man. Man's destiny is to express God in all sorts of glorious ways. To express means to press outward, or bring into sight. Every feature of your life is really a manifestation or expression of something in your soul.

Since it is misunderstandings about the relationship of God and man that lead to all our difficulties, it is worth any amount of trouble to correctly understand that relationship. Trying to have manifestation without Cause is atheism and materialism, and we know where they lead. "Our Father which art in heaven."

. . . as God hath said, I will dwell in them, and walk in them . . . (2 Corinthians 6:16).

If we trace the derivation of the word *hallowed* we will discover a most extraordinarily significant fact. The word *hallowed* has the same root as *holy, whole, wholesome,* and *heal,* or *healed;* so we see that the nature of God is complete and perfect—altogether good. Some very remarkable consequences follow from this fact. We have agreed that an effect must be similar in its nature to its cause, and so, because the nature of God is hallowed, everything that is projected by that Cause must be hallowed or perfect too. God cannot cause or send anything but perfect good. God cannot, as people sometimes think, send sickness or trouble, or accidents—much less death—for these things are unlike His nature.

Thou art of purer eyes than to behold evil, and canst not look on iniquity . . . (Habakkuk 1:13).

Thy kingdom come (Matthew 6:10).

Man, being manifestation or expression of God, has a limitless destiny before him. His work is to express, in concrete, definite form, the ideas that God furnishes him, and in order to do this, he must have creative power. Elsewise, he would be merely a machine through which God worked—an automaton. But man, having the nature of his father, remains a creator. Notice that the word *individual* means "undivided." The consciousness of man is not separated from God's consciousness.

"Thy kingdom come" means that it is our duty to bring more and more of God's ideas into concrete manifestation upon this plane. That is what we are here for. The old saying, "God has a plan for every man, and he has one for you," is quite correct.

If only you can find out the thing God intends you to do, and will do it, you will find that all doors will open to you, and you will be gloriously happy. There is a true place in life for each one of us where we can bring the Kingdom of God into manifestation, and truly say, "Thy Kingdom cometh."

Thy will be done on earth, as it is in heaven (Matthew 6:10).

Now we too often choose to use our free will in a negative way; allowing ourselves to think selfishly, and this wrong thinking brings upon us all our troubles. Instead of understanding that it is our essential nature to express God, to be ever about our Father's business, we try to set up our own account. We abuse our own free will, trying to work apart from God; and the very natural result is all the sickness, poverty, sin, trouble, and death that we find on the physical plane. We must never for a moment try to make plans or arrangements without reference to God, or suppose that we can be either happy or successful if we are seeking any other end than to do his Will.

Our business is to bring our whole nature as fast as we can into conformity with the will of God. "In his will is our peace," said Dante, and the *Divine Comedy* is really a study in fundamental states of consciousness, the Inferno representing the state of the soul that is endeavoring to live without God, the Paradiso representing the state of the soul that has achieved its conscious unity with the divine Will. It was this sublime conflict of the soul that wrung from the heart of the great Augustine the cry, "Thou hast made us for Thyself, and our hearts are restless until they find themselves in Thee."

G*ive us this day our daily bread* (Matthew 6:11).

Because we are the children of a loving Father, we are entitled to expect that God will provide us with everything we need. If we do so expect, in faith and understanding, we shall never look in vain.

It is the will of God that we should all lead healthy, happy lives, full of joyous experience; that we should develop freely and steadily. To this end we require such things as food, clothing, shelter, means of travel, books, and so on; above all, we require freedom. In the Prayer all these things are included under the heading of bread; that is to say, not merely food in general, but all things required for a healthy, free, and harmonious life. But in order to obtain these things we have to claim them, and we have to recognize God alone as the source and fountainhead of all our good. Lack of any kind is always traceable to the fact that we have been seeking our supply from some secondary source, instead of from God himself, the author and giver of life.

People think of their supply as coming from certain investments, or from a business, or from an employer, perhaps; whereas these are merely the channels through which it comes, God being the Source. A particular channel is likely to change, because change is the cosmic law for manifestation. Stagnation is really death; but as long as you realize that the Source of your supply is the one unchangeable Spirit, all is well. The fading out of one channel will be but the signal for the opening of another.

In its inner and most important meaning, our daily bread signifies the realization of the Presence of God—an actual sense that God exists not merely in a nominal way, but as *the* great reality; we can rely upon Him to supply all that we need to have; teach us all that we need to know; and guide our steps so that we shall not make mistakes. This is Emanuel, or God with us.

But my God shall supply all your need . . . (Philippians 4:19).

The common mistake, of course, is to suppose that a formal recognition of God is sufficient, or that talking about divine things is the same as possessing them; but this is exactly on a par with supposing that looking at a tray of food, or discussing the chemical composition of sundry foodstuffs, is the same thing as actually eating a meal. It is this mistake that is responsible for the fact that people sometimes pray for a thing for years without any tangible result. If prayer is a force at all, it cannot be possible to pray without something happening. Pray regularly and quietly—remember that in all mental work, effort or strain defeats itself—then presently, the realization will come.

Another reason why the symbol of bread for the experience of the Presence of God is such a telling one, is that the act of eating food is essentially a thing that must be done for oneself. No one can assimilate food for another. In the same way, the realization of the Presence of God is a thing that no one else can have for us.

For he satisfieth the longing soul, and filleth the hungry soul with goodness (Psalm 107:9).

In speaking of the "bread of life," Jesus calls it our *daily* bread. The reason for this is very fundamental—our contact with God must be a living one. It is our momentary attitude that governs our being.

. . . behold, now is the accepted time; behold, now is the day of salvation (2 Corinthians 6:2).

The most futile thing in the world is to seek to live upon a past realization. The thing that means spiritual life to you is your realization of God *here* and *now*.

Be thankful for yesterday's experience, knowing that it is with you forever in the change of consciousness that it brought about, but do not lean upon it for a single moment for the need of today. The manna in the desert is the Old Testament prototype of this daily nourishment. The people wandering in the wilderness were told that they would be supplied with manna from heaven every day but they were on no account to try to save it up for the morrow. When, notwithstanding the rule, some of them did try to live upon yesterday's food, the result was pestilence or death.

So it is with us. The art of life is to live in the present moment, and to make that moment as perfect as we can by the realization that we are the instruments and expression of God Himself.

Forgive us our trespasses, as we forgive them that trespass against us (Matthew 6:12).

This clause is the turning point of the Prayer. It is the strategic key. Having told us what God is, what man is, how the universe works, how we are to do our own work, what our true nourishment or supply is, and the way in which we can obtain it, he now comes to the forgiveness of sins.

The forgiveness of sins is the central problem of life. Sin is a sense of separation from God, and is the major tragedy of human experience. It is, of course, rooted in selfishness. It is essentially an attempt to gain some supposed good to which we are not entitled in justice. It is a sense of isolated, self-regarding, personal existence, whereas the Truth of Being is that all is One. Our true selves are at one with God, undivided from Him, expressing His ideas, witnessing to His nature. Because we are all one with the great Whole of which we are spiritually a part, it follows that we are one with all men.

Evil, sin, the fall of man, in fact, is essentially the attempt to negate this Truth. We try to live apart from God. We act as though we could have plans and purposes and interests separate from Him. All this, if it were true, would mean that existence is not one and harmonious, but a chaos of competition and strife. But, of course, it is not true, and therein lies the joy of life.

As we repeat the Great Prayer intelligently, we are suddenly caught up and grasped as though in a vise, so that we must face this problem of separation from God. We must extend forgiveness to everyone.

Notice that Jesus does not say, "Forgive me my trespasses and I will try to forgive others." He obliges us to declare that we have actually forgiven, *and he makes our claim to our forgiveness to depend upon that.* Who could be so insane as to endeavor to seek the Kingdom of God without desiring to be relieved of his own sense of guilt? We are trapped in the inescapable position that we cannot demand our own release before we have released our brother.

Search me, O God, and know my heart: try me, and know my thoughts (Psalm 139:23).

And *as ye would that men should do to you, do ye also to them like-wise* (Luke 6:31).

The forgiveness of others is the vestibule of Heaven. You have to get rid of all resentment and condemnation of others, and, not least, of self-condemnation and remorse. You have to forgive yourself, but you cannot forgive yourself sincerely until you have forgiven others first.

Of course, nothing in all the world is easier than to forgive people who have not hurt us very much. But what the Law of Being requires of us is that we forgive the very things that are so hard to forgive that at first it seems impossible to do it at all. But the Lord's Prayer makes our own escape from guilt and limitation dependent upon just this very thing.

If your prayers are not being answered, search your consciousness and see if there is not some old circumstance about which you are still resentful. Search and see if you are not really holding a grudge against some individual, or some group. If so, then you have an act of forgiveness to perform, and when this is done, you will probably make your demonstration. If you cannot forgive at present, you will have to wait for your demonstration until you can, and you will have to postpone finishing your recital of the Lord's Prayer too.

If ye forgive men their trespasses, your heavenly Father will also forgive you (Matthew 6:14).

Setting others free means setting yourself free, because resentment is really a form of attachment. It is a cosmic truth that it takes two to make a prisoner; a prisoner and a jailer. There is no such thing as being a prisoner on one's own account. Moreover, the jailer is as much a prisoner as his charge. When you hold resentment against anyone, you are bound to that person by a mental chain. You are tied by a cosmic tie to the thing that you hate. The one person perhaps in the whole world whom you most dislike is the very one to whom you are attaching yourself by a hook that is stronger than steel. Is this what you wish? Is this the condition in which you desire to go on living? Remember, you belong to the thing with which you are linked in thought, and at some time or other, if that tie endures, the object of your resentment will be drawn again into your life, perhaps to work further havoc. No one can afford such a thing; and so you must cut all such ties by a clear act of forgiveness. You must loose him and let him go. By forgiveness you set yourself free; you save your soul. And because the law of love works alike for one and all, you help to save his soul too.

C*ast thy burden upon the Lord, and he shall sustain thee* . . . (Psalm 55:22).

The technique of forgiveness is not very difficult when you understand how. The only thing that is essential is willingness to forgive. Provided you desire to forgive the offender, the greatest part of the work is already done.

The method of forgiving is this: Get by yourself and become quiet. Repeat any prayer that appeals to you, or read a chapter of the Bible. Then quietly say, "I fully and freely forgive X (mentioning the name of the offender); I loose him and let him go. I cast the burden aside. He is free now, and I am free too. The Truth of Christ has set us both free. I thank God."

On no account repeat this act of forgiveness, because to do it a second time would be tacitly to repudiate your own work. Afterward, whenever the memory of the offender or the offense happens to come into your mind, bless the delinquent briefly and dismiss the thought. Do this, however many times the thought may come back. You will find that all bitterness and resentment have disappeared, and you are both free with the perfect freedom of the children of God. Your forgiveness is complete.

Lead us not into temptation; but deliver us from evil (Matthew 6:13).

Many earnest people feel that God could not lead anyone into temptation in any circumstances, and that Jesus could not have said what he is represented to have said, and so some other phrasing is sought more in accordance with the general tone of his teaching. All this, however, is unnecessary.

The facts are these—the more you pray, the more sensitive you become, and the more powerful are your prayers. But you also become susceptible to forms of temptation that simply do not beset those at an earlier stage. Subtle and powerful temptations await; temptations to work for self-glory, for personal distinction; temptation to personal preferences other than perfect impartiality. Beyond all other temptations the deadly sin of spiritual pride. Many who have surmounted all other testings have lapsed into self-righteousness that has fallen like a curtain of steel between them and God.

Some old writers were so vividly sensible of these dangers that they spoke of the soul as being challenged by various tests as it traversed the upward road. The traveler was halted at various turnpike bars, and tested by some ordeal to determine whether he were ready to advance any further. If he succeeded in passing the test he was allowed to continue upon his way with the blessing of the challenger.

Now, some less experienced souls, eager for rapid advancement, have rashly desired to be subjected immediately to all kinds of tests, and have even looked about, seeking for difficulties to overcome. Forgetting our Lord's injunction *Thou shalt not tempt the Lord thy God* (Matthew 4:7), they have virtually challenged him to give them difficulties. And so Jesus has inserted this clause, in which we pray that we may not have to meet anything that is too much for us at the present level of our understanding.

Thine is the kingdom, and the power, and the glory, for ever and ever (Matthew 6:13).

This is a wonderful gnomic saying summing up the essential truth of the Omnipresence and the Allness of God.

We know that God is the only power, and so, when we work, it is really God working by means of us. Just as the pianist produces his music by means of, or through his fingers, so may mankind be thought of as the fingers of God. His is the Power. If, when you have anything to do, you hold the thought, "Divine Intelligence is working through me now," you will perform the most difficult tasks.

The wondrous change that comes over us as we gradually realize what the Omnipresence of God really means, transfigures every phase of our lives, turning sorrow into joy, age into youth, and dullness into light and life. This is the glory!

God intended us to have dominion over our lives, to be the captains of our souls.

Of course, in the ship of life, you cannot make port unless all sails are set. You must pursue the spiritual life wholeheartedly. You cannot expect to reach port if you are faithful in your prayers and meditations for a time, and then for a time you forget God.

You are the captain of your soul when you can say with Jesus,

I and my Father are one (John 10:30).

. . . the Father that dwelleth in me, he doeth the works (John 14:10).

When you are praying or "treating" about a particular thing, you should handle it, mentally, very carefully indeed. The ideal way is not to think about it at all except when you are actually praying about it. Moreover, to talk to other people about it is exceedingly likely to invite failure.

When a new problem presents itself to you, decline to consider it except in the light of Truth. I call this "putting a subject in quarantine." Even an old long-standing problem can be "put in quarantine" today, if you mean business and will resolutely break the habit of constantly thinking over that problem.

Whenever you think about any subject, you are treating it with your thought—either for good or evil.

The lip of truth shall be established for ever . . . (Proverbs 12:19).

Man is a mental being, and to know this is the first step on the road to freedom and prosperity, for as long as you believe yourself to be primarily physical, a superior kind of animal, you will remain in bondage—in bondage, that is to say, to your own habits of thought, for there is no other bondage.

Since you are a mental being, you will see how foolish it is for you to endeavor to improve your conditions by altering your environment while leaving your mind unchanged. To attempt this is to foredoom yourself to disappointment. Mind is cause, and experience is effect. If you do not like the experience or effect that you are getting, the obvious remedy is to alter the cause and then the effect will naturally alter too.

Thou blind Pharisee, cleanse first that which is within the cup and platter, that the outside of them may be clean also (Matthew 23:26).

There is an anecdote of the Far West that carries a wonderful lesson. It appears that a party of hunters, being called away from their camp, left the campfire unattended, with a kettle of water boiling on it.

Presently an old bear crept out of the woods, and, seeing the kettle with its lid dancing about on top, promptly seized it. The boiling water scalded him badly; but instead of dropping the kettle instantly, he proceeded to hug it tightly—this being a bear's idea of defense. Of course, the tighter he hugged it the more it burned him; and the more it burned him the tighter he hugged it; and so on in a vicious circle, to the undoing of the bear.

This illustrates perfectly the way in which many people hug their difficulties to their bosoms by constantly rehearsing them to themselves and others.

Whenever you catch yourself thinking about your grievances, say to yourself sternly: "Bear hugs kettle," and think about God instead. You will be surprised how quickly some long-standing wounds will heal.

Mine eyes are ever toward the Lord . . . (Psalm 25:15).

You think, and your thoughts materialize as experience, and thus it is, all unknown to yourself as a rule, that you are actually weaving the pattern of your own destiny, here and now, by the way in which you allow yourself to think, day by day and all day long.

Your fate is largely in your own hands. Nobody but yourself can keep you down. Neither parents, nor wives, nor husbands, nor employers, nor neighbors; nor poverty, nor ignorance, nor any power whatever can keep you out of your own when once you have learned how to think.

For I am persuaded, that neither death, nor life, nor angels, nor principalities, nor powers, nor things present, nor things to come,

Nor height, nor depth, nor any other creature, shall be able to separate us from the love of God, which is in Christ Jesus our Lord (Romans 8:38–39).

The principal revelation of the Jesus Christ teaching is the omnipresence and availability of God, and the belief that God not only transcends His universe but is everywhere immanent in it—that He indwells in it.

If you really believe in the existence of God you should be happy and cheerful. God has all power, and God is good; so life must be good too.

Meet the world with a smile. You owe this to God, to your fellows, and above all, to yourself. If you go about with a face like an east wind, what can you possibly expect to attract from the world? We all know people who carry a fixed, frozen, mirthless, almost professional, smile. Such a smile is just a permanent wave in the face.

Smile, even if it takes a little effort, and keep it up until it becomes spontaneous, as it will. In the graphic language of Hollywood, *register joy, and hold it!*

For ye shall go out with joy . . . (Isaiah 55:12).

An understanding faith is the life of prayer. It is a great mistake, however, to struggle to produce a lively faith within yourself. That can only end in failure. The thing to do is to act as though you had faith. Act out what you wish to demonstrate, and you will be expressing true faith. This is the right use of the will, scientifically understood.

   . . . *Verily I say unto you, if ye have faith, and doubt not, ye shall not only do this which is done to the fig tree, but also if ye shall say unto this mountain, Be thou removed, and be thou cast into the sea, it shall be done* (Matthew 21:21).

   This statement of Jesus is perhaps the most tremendous spiritual pronouncement ever made. Jesus knew the law of faith and proved it many times. We shall move mountains when we are willing to believe that we can, and then not only will mountains be moved, but the whole planet will be redeemed and re-formed according to the Pattern in the Mount.

. . . *be ye transformed by the renewing of your mind* . . . (Romans 12:2).

This is Paul's admonition.

Many people understand this in principle, but they fail to demonstrate because they do not carry it out logically in practice. During prayer, they carefully build up the new mental structure, but as soon as their time of prayer is over, instead of faithfully preserving that structure intact they promptly knock it down again by negative thinking. Obviously, a bricklayer could work hard in this fashion year after year without ever accomplishing anything.

If you are failing to demonstrate, it is probably due to the same cause—building followed by wrecking. We are transformed by the *renewing* of our minds.

The moment you catch yourself thinking a negative thought, you should reject it instantly. Do not stop to say "good-by" to the error but immediately switch your attention to the Presence of God. Indeed, we may say that when error presents itself to consciousness, the first five seconds are golden.

When ye therefore shall see the abomination of desolation, spoken of by Daniel the prophet, stand in the holy place (whoso readeth, let him understand:)

Then let them which be in Judea flee into the mountains;

Let him which is on the housetop not come down to take any thing out of his house;

Neither let him which is in the field return back to take his clothes (Matthew 24:15–18).

Jesus teaches this lesson in his own graphic way. The holy place is your consciousness, and the abomination of desolation is any negative thought, because a negative thought means belief in the absence of God at the point concerned.

It is impossible to forget this illustration once we have taken it in.

Most people have certain sections of their lives where, for various reasons (mostly unknown to themselves), they do not wish to make any change. These places are set aside and surrounded with an aura of spurious sanctity like the sacred cows of the East, which are considered too holy to be touched. But if you really mean business about regenerating your soul and body, there must positively be no sacred cows in your life.

Nothing is truly sacred but your own Indwelling Christ and the process of His awakening.

. . . *Awake thou that sleepest, and arise from the dead, and Christ shall give thee light* (Ephesians 5:14).

It cannot be your duty to do anything that is beyond your reach or your strength at the moment.

It cannot be your duty to do anything that sacrifices your own integrity or your own spiritual development.

It cannot be right to be hurried, or sad, or discouraged, or angry, or resentful, or antagonistic, under any circumstances.

If you have no time for prayer and meditation, you will have lots of time for sickness and trouble.

Let us hear the conclusion of the whole matter: Fear God, and keep his commandments: for this is the whole duty of man (Ecclesiastes 12:13).

There is nothing in the universe that you cannot do or be if you are mentally ready. People speak of golden opportunities but what we call opportunity is really our own mental readiness. Napoleon said, "Opportunities? I make opportunities"; and while this would be merely a vainglorious boast for one who is not on the spiritual basis, yet when you do understand the Truth of Being, it is simply a statement of fact. The Romans could have had the telephone; the Greeks could have had the cinema; the Babylonians could have had the automobile—had they been mentally ready. The laws of nature were the same in those ages as in ours, the same materials were in the ground—but the minds of the Ancients were not ready for those things, and so they had to go without them.

Supply the necessary mental condition, and the demand, the opportunity, or the occasion, will present itself automatically.

Whenever you are ready you will find that everything else is ready too.

Take ye heed, watch and pray: for ye know not when the time is (Mark 13:33).

To recognize failure intelligently is the first step toward building success.

Recognize success with thanksgiving, and build more success on that.

You can have anything in life that you really want, but you must be prepared to take the responsibilities that go with it.

God is ready the moment you are.

You really do not know John Smith; you only know the idea that you form of John Smith.

One God and Father of all, who is above all, and through all, and in you all (Ephesians 4:6).

Don't wait about for God to act dramatically—because He probably won't. When people expect a dramatic miracle from the outside, they are really hoping to change conditions without changing themselves; to get something for nothing, in fact, and that would be a violation of cosmic law.

Don't wait for God to tell you what to do from the outside—He won't.

And the Lord direct your hearts into the love of God, and into the patient waiting for Christ (2 Thessalonians 3:5).

Have you an open mind? Is the window of your soul open for fresh air and the sunshine of Truth to come in, or is it closed and shuttered by mental laziness or the emotional congestion that we call prejudice?

None of us knows how many fine things we have missed through being self-satisfied and cocksure. No one can be considered really intelligent who does not have a readiness to examine new ideas with an open mind.

The history of scientific discovery shows that almost every new step was opposed by the very people who should have welcomed it.

Harvey was denounced for claiming that the blood circulated through the body; Galileo was persecuted for saying that the earth went round the sun; Pasteur was branded a quack for advancing the germ theory of disease; Jenner was threatened with the police for pioneering vaccination. The finality of the atom, which was a scientific dogma in the childhood of most of us, has been completely discarded.

Probably the only incorrigible fool is the man who says that anything is impossible, or that there is any limit to the conquests that divine Intelligence working in mankind can achieve.

The Lord is able to give thee much more than this (2 Chronicles 25:9).

Sit down quietly where you are not likely to be disturbed. Relax the body—and begin to think about *yourself*. Every time your thought wanders to something higher, bring it back gently but relentlessly.

Think about the past. Think over all the mistakes you have made, going right back to childhood. Think over all the opportunities you have missed and the time you have wasted. Especially think of all the occasions upon which you have been badly treated.

Think about your body and wonder if your age or your job or the climate isn't beginning to tell. See if you cannot discover a pain or an ache somewhere.

Think about finances and if they are going well now, insist that this is probably too good to last.

In any case, think about *yourself*, that is the main point, and if you will keep this up faithfully for fifteen or twenty minutes, there can be no doubt about the result.

Seest thou a man wise in his own conceit? There is more hope of a fool than of him (Proverbs 26:12).

Knock everything systematically. No matter what you hear of, deprecate it and predict the worst.

Mind everyone else's business. This will insure your neglecting your own.

Never perform today what you can possibly postpone until tomorrow.

Leave the important things to someone else instead of seeing to them personally.

Have no organized arrangements. Trust to luck for everything.

Be a sanctimonious humbug, and when you bungle things say it is "the Lord's will" or that the trouble is that you are too good for your surroundings.

Sit down and wait for something to turn up.

Finally, conduct your life in all respects as if there were no God.

Deliver me from all my transgressions: make me not the reproach of the foolish (Psalm 39:8).

Never be original. Find out what is usually done and copy that.

Realize that you have nothing more to learn. This will destroy all danger of success.

Sneer at those who are more successful than yourself.

Tell yourself that it is now too late, and that you really did not have the proper equipment; and it will be especially helpful to keep saying that people are against you.

Never learn from experience. Keep on doing the same fool things time after time.

Never wait to hear the other side of the story. Knowing both sides will only unsettle your mind.

Use your wit destructively. Be smart at the expense of absent people.

Stand on your dignity. Never forget that you have a position to keep up.

Try to get everything cheap. Study and practice to become the perfect "chiseler." This will build an invincible poverty complex.

. . . *the heart of fools proclaimeth foolishness* (Proverbs 12:23).

Get emotional and excited over every trifling occurrence, especially if it is no concern of yours.

Eat and drink indiscriminately. Your stomach is only a sink, anyway, and being made of cast iron, will stand anything.

Cut down your sleep. This is an excellent way to undermine the nervous system.

Never relax. That would give the body a chance to recuperate.

Avoid all exercise. Exercise promotes circulation.

Read as much as you can about diseases and ailments. Your public library will carry many suitable books.

Discuss your own ailments at great length and, if you have had an operation, give dramatic little lectures about it at every opportunity.

Take good care of your dog, and your horse, and your automobile, but neglect your body. The Bible says that your body is the Temple of the Holy Spirit, and to go against the Bible is always a good shortcut to trouble.

. . . If thou wilt diligently hearken to the voice of the Lord thy God, and wilt do that which is right in his sight, and wilt give ear to his commandments, and keep all his statutes, I will put none of these diseases upon thee . . . for I am the Lord that healeth thee (Exodus 15:26).

Treatment is a psycho-spiritual term that means knowing the spiritual truth about any person or situation.

If, like most people, you believe that appearances are realities and that they cannot be changed, then you cannot give a treatment. But if you believe that the Bible is right when it says,

For as he thinketh in his heart, so is he . . . (Proverbs 23:7).

Judge not according to the appearance, but judge righteous judgment (John 7:24).

Then it is in your power to change anything for the better and to heal most things.

Begin every treatment (no matter how many you may give) by saying:

I can overcome this difficulty.

C*ast thy burden upon the Lord, and he shall sustain thee: he shall never suffer the righteous to be moved* (Psalm 55:22).

We sometimes hear the expression used, "cast the burden," and it is useful to consider what this phrase really means. Used intelligently, it is one of the great keys to spiritual victory. To cast the burden means really to insist upon harmony and peace of mind, and to cease from worry and anxiety there and then.

If, when you are faced with trouble, whether it be old or new, you can affirm positively the harmony of being and then refuse to re-open the case, no matter how much fear may urge you to do so, you *have cast your burden upon the Lord,* and you will win.

The study of the Bible is not unlike the search for diamonds in South Africa. At first people found a few diamonds in the yellow clay, and they were delighted with their good fortune, even while they supposed that this was to be the full extent of their find. Then, upon digging deeper, they came upon the blue clay, and to their amazement found as many precious stones in a day as they had previously found in a year.

In your exploration of Bible Truth, see to it that you do not rest satisfied in the yellow clay of a few spiritual discoveries, but press on to the rich blue clay underneath. The Bible, however, differs from the diamond field in the sublime fact that beneath the blue clay there are more and still more and richer strata, awaiting the touch of spiritual perception—on and on to Infinity.

O the depth of the riches both of the wisdom and knowledge of God! how unsearchable are his judgments, and his ways past finding out! (Romans 11:33).

Jesus Christ is easily the most important figure that has ever appeared in the history of mankind. This is true whether you choose to call him God or man. His life and death and teachings have influenced the course of human history more than those of any other man who ever lived. There can hardly, therefore, be a more important undertaking than to inquire into the question of what Jesus really did stand for.

What did Jesus teach? What did he really wish us to believe and to do? How far does the Christianity of today present his message to the world? What *did* Jesus teach?

. . . *for, behold, the kingdom of God is within you* (Luke 17:21).

This is my commandment, That ye love one another, as I have loved you (John 15:12).

If ye shall ask any thing in my name, I will do it (John 14:14).

Jesus explains what the nature of God is, and what our own nature is; tells us the meaning of life and of death; shows us why we make mistakes; why we yield to temptation; why we become sick, and impoverished, and old; and, most important of all, he tells us how all these evils may be overcome, and how we may bring fulfillment into our lives, and into the lives of others.

Jesus warns us, not once but often, that obstinacy in sin can bring very severe punishment, and that a man who parts with the integrity of his soul—even though he gain the whole world—is a tragic fool. But he teaches that we are only punished for—and actually punished by—our own mistakes; and he teaches that every man or woman, no matter how steeped in evil and uncleanness, has always direct access to an all-loving, all-powerful Father-God, who will forgive him, and supply His own strength to him to enable him to find himself again.

If ye know that he is righteous, ye know that every one that doeth righteousness is born of him (1 John 2:29).

Jesus made a special point of discouraging the laying of emphasis upon outer observances; and, indeed, upon hard-and-fast rules and regulations of every kind. What he insisted upon was a certain spirit in one's conduct, knowing that when the spirit is right, details will take care of themselves. Yet, in spite of this, the history of orthodox Christianity is largely made up of attempts to enforce all sorts of external observances upon the people.

Who also hath made us able ministers of the new testament; not of the letter, but of the spirit: for the letter killeth, but the spirit giveth life (2 Corinthians 3:6).

Jesus taught through miracles.

If the miracles did not happen, the rest of the Gospel story loses all real significance. If Jesus did not believe them to be possible, and undertake to perform them, then the Gospel message is chaotic, contradictory, and devoid of significance.

But the deeds related to Jesus in the Four Gospels did happen, and many others too, "the which, if they should be written, every one, I suppose that even the world itself could not contain the books that should be written." Jesus himself justified what people thought to be a strange teaching by the works he was able to do; and he went further and said,

. . . the works that I do shall he do also; and greater works . . . (John 14:12).

Now what, after all, is a miracle? Those who deny the possibility of miracles on the ground that the universe is a perfect system of law and order, to the operation of which there can be no exceptions, are perfectly right. But the explanation is that the world of which we are normally aware, and with whose laws alone most people are acquainted, is only a fragment of the whole universe as it really is; and that there is such a thing as appealing from a lower to a higher law—from a lesser to a greater expression. In the sense of a real breach of law, miracles are impossible. Yet, in the sense that all ordinary rules and limitations of the physical plane can be set aside or overridden by an understanding that has risen about them, miracles can and do happen.

Let us suppose, for the sake of example, that on a certain Monday, your affairs are in such a condition that, humanly speaking, certain consequences are sure to follow before the end of the week. These may be legal consequences, perhaps of a very unpleasant nature following upon some decision of the courts; or a physician may decide that a perilous operation will be necessary. Now, if someone can raise the consciousness of the harassed individual above the limitations of the physical plane then the conditions on that plane will change, and, in some unforeseen and normally impossible manner, the legal tragedy will melt away, and to the advantage, be it noted, of all parties to the case; or the patient will be healed instead of having to undergo the operation.

In other words, miracles, in the popular sense of the word, can and do happen as the result of a change of consciousness, and a change of consciousness is usually accomplished through prayer. Thus prayer does change things.

For as the heavens are higher than the earth, so are my ways higher than your ways, and my thoughts than your thoughts (Isaiah 55:9).

Externally, the Bible is a collection of inspired documents written by men of all kinds, in all sorts of circumstances, and over hundreds of years of time. The documents are seldom originals, but redactions and compilations of older fragments; and the names of the actual writers are seldom known for certain. This, however, does not affect the spiritual purpose of the Bible. The book, as we have it, is an inexhaustible reservoir of spiritual Truth, compiled under divine inspiration, and the actual route by which it reached its present form does not matter.

History, biography, lyrical and other poetic forms are various mediums through which the spiritual message is given in the Bible; and, above all, the parable is used to convey spiritual and metaphysical truth. In some cases what was never intended to be more than a parable was, at one time, taken for literal statement of fact; and this often made the Bible seem to teach things that are opposed to common sense.

The spiritual key to the Bible rescues us from these difficulties, dilemmas, and seeming inconsistencies. And the Truth turns out to be nothing less than the amazing but undeniable fact that the whole outer world—whether it be the physical body, the common things of life, the winds and the rain, the clouds, the earth itself—is amenable to man's thought, and that he has dominion over it when he knows it.

Thou madest him to have dominion over the works of thy hands; thou hast put all things under his feet (Psalm 8:6).

Truth never changes, but what we have to deal with on this plane is man's apprehension of the Truth, and throughout historical time, this has been steadily and continuously becoming more plain to us.

Jesus Christ summed up this Truth, taught it completely and thoroughly, and, above all, demonstrated it in his own person. Most of us now can glimpse intellectually the idea of what it must mean in its fullness. To accept the Truth is the great first step, but not until we have proved it in doing is it ours. Jesus proved everything that he taught, even to the overcoming of death in what we call the resurrection. By surmounting every sort of limitation to which mankind is subject, he performed a work of unique and incalculable value to the race, and is therefore justly entitled the Savior of the world.

. . . when he, the Spirit of truth, is come, he will guide you into all truth . . . (John 16:13).

The setting forth of the Sermon on the Mount is an almost perfect codification of the religion of Jesus Christ. It covers the essentials. It is practical and personal. It is definite, specific, and yet widely illuminating. Once the true meaning of the instructions has been grasped, it is only necessary to begin putting them into practice to get immediate results. The magnitude and extent of these results will depend solely upon the sincerity and thoroughness with which they are applied. That is a matter which each individual has to settle for himself.

If you really do wish to become a different person altogether in the sight of God and man, then Jesus, in his Sermon on the Mount, has clearly shown you how it is to be done.

If you are prepared to break with the old man, and start upon the creation of the new one, then the study of the great Sermon will indeed be to you the Mountain of Liberation.

But be ye doers of the word, and not hearers only, deceiving your own selves (James 1:22).

The Sermon on the Mount opens with the eight Beatitudes. They are actually a prose poem in eight verses and constitute a general summary of the Christian teaching. A general summing up, such as this, is highly characteristic of the old Oriental mode of approach to a religious and philosophical teaching, and it naturally recalls the Eightfold Path of Buddhism, the Ten Commandments of Moses, and other such compact groupings of ideas.

Jesus concerned himself exclusively with the teaching of general principles, and these general principles always had to do with mental states, for he knew that if one's mental states are right, everything else might be right too. Unlike the other great religious teachers, he gives us no detailed instructions about what we are to do or are not to do.

. . . *the hour cometh, when ye shall neither in this mountain, nor yet at Jerusalem, worship the Father.*

. . . *the hour cometh, and now is, when the true worshippers shall worship the Father in spirit and in truth: for the Father seeketh such to worship him.*

God is a Spirit: and they that worship him must worship him in spirit and in truth (John 4:21, 23–24).

Blessed are the poor in spirit: for theirs is the kingdom of heaven (Matthew 5:3).

To be poor in spirit does not in the least mean the thing we call "poor spirited." To be poor in spirit means to have emptied yourself of all desire to exercise personal self-will, and, what is just as important, to have renounced all preconceived opinions in the whole-hearted search for God. It means to be willing to set aside your present habits of thought, your present views and prejudices, your present way of life if necessary; to jettison, in fact, anything and everything that can stand in the way of your finding God.

One of the saddest passages in all literature is the story of the Rich Young Man who missed one of the great opportunities of history, and

. . . *went away sorrowful: for he had great possessions* (Matthew 19:22).

This is really the story of mankind in general. We reject the salvation that Jesus offers us—our chance of finding God—because we "have great possessions"; not so much that we are very rich in terms of money, for indeed most people are not, but because we have great possessions in the way of preconceived ideas—confidence in our own judgment, and in the ideas with which we happen to be familiar. We have pride, born of academic distinction; sentimental or material attachment to institutions and organizations; habits of life that we have no desire to renounce; concern for human respect; or perhaps fear of public ridicule. And these possessions keep us chained to the rock of suffering that is our exile from God.

The *poor in spirit* suffer from none of these embarrassments, either because they never had them, or because they have risen above them on the tide of spiritual understanding.

Blessed are they that mourn: for they shall be comforted (Matthew 5:4).

Mourning or sorrow is not in itself a good thing, for the will of God is that everyone should experience happiness and joyous success. Jesus says:

. . . *I am come that they might have life, and that they might have it more abundantly* (John 10:10).

Nevertheless, trouble and suffering are often extremely useful, because many people will not bother to learn the Truth until driven to do so by sorrow and failure. Sorrow then becomes relatively a good thing. Sooner or later every human being will have to discover the truth about God, and make his own contact with Him at first hand. He will have to acquire the understanding of Truth, which will set him free, once and for all, from our three-dimensional limitations and their concomitants—sin, sickness, and death. There is really no need for man to have trouble, because if he will only seek God first, the trouble need never come. He always has the choice of learning by spiritual unfoldment or of learning by painful experience. Family troubles, quarrels and estrangements, sin and remorse, need never come at all if we seek first the Kingdom of God and Right Understanding; but if we will not do so, then come they must, and for us this mourning will be a blessing in disguise, for through it we shall be "comforted." And by comfort the Bible means the experience of the Presence of God, which is the end of all mourning.

Blessed are the meek: for they shall inherit the earth (Matthew 5:5).

On the surface, this Beatitude seems to be contradicted by the facts of everyday life. But either Jesus knew what he was talking about, and is to be taken seriously, or his teaching should be dropped altogether. If he is to be relied upon, then let us pay him the compliment of assuming that he knew best about the art of living.

The fact is that when correctly understood, the teaching of Jesus is found to be the most practicable of all doctrines; and the whole essence of his teaching and of its application is summed up in this text. When you possess the spiritual meaning of this text you have the secret of dominion—the secret of overcoming every kind of difficulty.

We notice that there are two polar words in the text—*meek* and *earth*. First of all, the word *earth* in the Bible really means the whole of your outer experience, and to "inherit the earth" means to have dominion over that outer experience. So we see that when the Bible talks about possessing the earth, governing the earth, making the earth glorious, it is referring to the conditions of our lives, from our bodily health outward to the farthest point in our affairs. So this text undertakes to tell us how we may possess, or govern, or be masters of our environment.

Let us see how we are to go about inheriting the earth. This Beatitude says that dominion, that is, power over the conditions of our lives, is to be obtained in a certain way, by nothing less than meekness.

The word *meek* in the Bible connotes a mental attitude for which there is no other single word available. It is a combination of open-mindedness, faith in God, and the realization that the will of God for us is always something joyous and interesting and vital. This state of mind also includes a perfect willingness to allow this will of God to come about in whatever way divine Wisdom considers to be best, rather than in some particular way that we have chosen for ourselves.

This mental attitude of teachableness, willingness to be led, is the key to dominion, or success in demonstration. There is no word for it in common speech, because the thing does not exist except for those who are up on the spiritual basis of the teaching of Jesus Christ. If we desire to inherit the earth we must absolutely acquire this "meekness."

The Lord reigneth; let the earth rejoice . . . (Psalm 97:1).

Moses—who overcame the old age belief to the extent of manifesting the physical body of a young man in the prime of life when, according to the calendar, he was one hundred and twenty years old, and then transcended matter altogether, or "dematerialized" without dying—was known preeminently for this quality; "as meek as Moses." Apart from his own personal demonstration, Moses also did a marvelous work for his whole nation, getting it out of Egyptian bondage in the face of incredible difficulties. Moses had an open mind, ready to be taught new things and new ways of thinking and working. He was not, in the beginning at least, free from serious faults of character, but he gradually rose above these defects as the new truth worked in his soul.

Moses thoroughly understood that to conform oneself rigorously to the will of God, far from involving the loss of any good, could only mean a better and more splendid life. He did not, therefore, think of his task as self-sacrifice, for he knew it to be the highest form of self-glorification—the glorification of God.

. . . *the Father that dwelleth in me, he doeth the works. . . . I am in the Father, and the Father in me* (John 14:10–11).

There is a marvelous Oriental saying that "meekness compels God himself."

Blessed are they which do hunger and thirst after righteousness: for they shall be filled (Matthew 5:6).

Righteousness is another of the key words of the Bible, one of those keys that the reader must have in his possession if he is to get at the true meaning of the book. Like *earth* and *meek* and *comfort*, it is used in a special and definite sense. Righteousness means not merely right conduct, but right thinking. In the Sermon on the Mount, every clause reiterates the truth that outer things are but consequences. *As within, so without.*

When people awaken to a knowledge of these truths, they naturally begin to apply them in their own lives. Realizing at last the vital importance of "righteousness" they begin immediately to try to put their house in order. The principle involved is simple, but unfortunately the exemplifying of it is anything but easy. Now, why should this be so? The answer lies in the potency of habit; and habits of thinking are at once the most subtle and the most difficult to break.

Perhaps failure to achieve righteousness is the failure of half-heartedness; you long but not too deeply. Your hunger and thirst do not rise from a sense of total need. Have a mental stocktaking or a review of your life. It could not happen that a wholehearted search for truth and righteousness, if persevered in, should not be crowned with success. God is not mocked, nor does He mock His children.

Blessed are the merciful: for they shall obtain mercy (Matthew 5:7).

This is a brief summary of the law of life that Jesus develops more fully later in the Sermon (Matthew 7:1–5). As it stands, this Beatitude is as obvious in its meaning as the law in question is simple and inflexible in its action.

The point that the Christian needs to note is that the principle covered in this Beatitude lies in its application to the realm of thought. Let us be merciful in our mental judgments of our brother, for, in truth, we are all one, and the more deeply he seems to err, the more urgent is the need for us to help him with the right thought, and so make it easier for him to get free.

Because in deed and in truth we are all one, component parts of the living garment of God, you yourself will ultimately receive the same treatment that you mete out to others; you will receive the same merciful help in your own hour of need from those who are farther along the path than you are.

Blessed are the pure in heart: for they shall see God (Matthew 5:8). This is one of those wonderful gnomic sayings in which the Bible is so rich. It is a summing up in a few words of a whole philosophy of religion.

Let us begin by considering what the promise in this Beatitude is. It is nothing less than to see God. To "see" in the sense referred to here, signifies spiritual perception, and spiritual perception is just that capacity to apprehend the true nature of Being that we all so sadly lack.

We live in God's world, but we do not in the least know it as it is. Heaven lies all about us—but because we are lacking in spiritual perception, we are unable to recognize it, to experience it, and, therefore, so far as we are concerned, we may be said to be shut out of Heaven.

We are very much in the position of a color-blind man in a beautiful flower garden. All around him are glorious colors; but he sees only blacks, whites, and grays. If we suppose him to be also devoid of the sense of smell, we shall see what a very small part of the glory of the garden exists for him. Yet it is all there, if he could but sense it.

Our task is to surmount these limitations as rapidly as may be, until we reach the point where we can know things as they really are—experience Heaven as it really is. That is what is meant by "seeing God." To see God is to apprehend Truth as it really is, and this is infinite freedom and perfect bliss.

. . . for they shall see God. In this wonderful Beatitude we are told exactly how this supreme task is to be accomplished and who they are who shall do it. They are the pure in heart. Purity, in its full and complete sense, is recognizing God alone as the only real Cause, and the only real Power in existence. It is what is called elsewhere in the Sermon "the single eye."

Note that Jesus speaks of the *pure in heart*. The word *heart* in the Bible usually means that part of man's mentality that modern psychology knows under the name of the "subconscious mind." This is exceedingly important because it is not sufficient for us to accept the Truth with the conscious mind only. At that stage it is still a mere opinion. It is not until it is accepted by the subconscious mind, and thus assimilated into the whole mentality, that it can make any difference in one's character or life.

. . . as he thinketh in his heart, so is he (Proverbs 23:7).

Keep thy heart with all diligence; for out of it are the issues of life (Proverbs 4:23).

Most people, and learned people especially, have all kinds of knowledge that does not in the least affect or improve their practical lives. Doctors know all about hygiene, but often live in an unhealthy way, notwithstanding; and philosophers, who are acquainted with the accumulated wisdom of the ages, and assent to most of it, continue to do foolish and stupid things in their own personal lives. Now, knowledge such as this is only opinion, or *head* knowledge, as some people call it. It has to become *heart* knowledge, or to be incorporated into the subconscious, before it can really change one. The modern psychologists in their efforts to "re-educate the subconscious" have the right idea, though they have not yet discovered the true method of doing so, which is by single-minded prayer, or the Practice of the Presence of God.

Jesus, of course, thoroughly understood all this, and that is why he stresses the fact that we have to be *pure in heart*.

Blessed are the peacemakers: for they shall be called the children of God (Matthew 5:9).

To the casual reader this Beatitude might sound like a mere conventional religious generalization, even a sententious platitude. Here we receive an invaluable practical lesson in the art of prayer—and prayer is our only means of returning to communion with God. As a matter of fact, prayer is the only real action in the full sense of the word, because prayer is the only thing that changes one's character. When such a change takes place, you become a different person and, therefore, for the rest of your life you act in a different way. If you should get a very strong realization of the Presence of God with you, it would make a very great and dramatic change in your character, so that, in the twinkling of an eye, your outlook, your habits, your whole life would completely change. Many such cases are on record, including cases of what used to be called "conversion." Because the change is radical, Jesus refers to it as being "born again."

The great essential for success in obtaining that sense of the Presence of God is that we first attain some degree of true peace of mind.

Peace I leave with you, my peace I give unto you. . . . Let not your heart be troubled, neither let it be afraid (John 14:27).

This true, interior soul-peace was known to the mystics as *serenity*, and they are never tired of telling us that serenity is the grand passport to the Presence of God—the sea as smooth as glass that is round about the Great White Throne. This is not to say that one cannot tackle even the most serious difficulties by prayer without having any serenity at all. But before you can make any true spiritual progress you must achieve serenity; and it is that fundamental tranquility of soul that Jesus refers to by the word *peace*—the peace that passes all human understanding.

The *Peacemakers* are those who bring about this peace in their own souls; they surmount limitation and become actually, not merely potentially, the *children of God*. This condition of mind is the objective at which Jesus aims.

Of course, to be a *peacemaker* in the usual sense of composing the quarrels of other people is an excellent thing; but, as all practical people know, an excessively difficult role to fill. But once you understand the power of prayer, you will be able to heal many quarrels in the true way; probably without speaking at all. The silent thought of the All-Power of Love and Wisdom will cause trouble to melt away almost imperceptibly. You will become a peacemaker.

Blessed are they which are persecuted for righteousness' sake: for theirs is the kingdom of heaven.

Blessed are ye, when men shall revile you, and persecute you, and shall say all manner of evil against you falsely, for my sake.

Rejoice, and be exceeding glad: for great is your reward in heaven: for so persecuted they the prophets which were before you (Matthew 5:10–12).

In view of what we know about the teaching of Jesus, that the will of God for us is harmony, peace, and joy, and that these things are to be attained by cultivating right thoughts, or "righteousness," this is a very startling statement. Jesus tells us again and again that it is our Father's good pleasure to give us the Kingdom, and that the way in which we are to receive it is by cultivating serenity, or peace of soul. He says that the peacemakers who do this, praying in "meekness" shall inherit the earth, have their mourning turned into joy, and that, in fact, whatever they shall ask the Father in the manner of this teaching, that will He do. Yet here we are told that it is blessed to be persecuted as the result of our "righteousness" for by this means we shall triumph; that it is cause for rejoicing and gladness to be reviled and accused; and that the prophets and Illumined Ones suffered these things too.

All this is indeed very startling, and it is perfectly correct. However, persecution only becomes an occasion for rejoicing when we are deeply aware of our real nature, our true immortality, and know that the suffering of our bodies can be transcended and even transmuted by our state of consciousness. Persecution can be for us a blessed condition when we realize that in such moments we are really advancing. . . . *be thou faithful unto death, and I will give thee a crown of life* (Revelation 2:10) is a promise that may become a reality right here on this earth.

GOLD

We know that the spiritual consciousness which we are all engaged in building is spoken of in the Bible as the Temple of Solomon. The name Solomon means peaceful, and symbolizes wisdom. This is logical, for peace of mind is the foundation of all spiritual building, the hallmark of understanding.

The Bible states that five things were to be found around the temple—*For the king had at sea a navy of Tharshish with the navy of Hiram: once in three years came the navy of Tharshish, bringing gold, and silver, ivory, and apes, and peacocks* (1 Kings 10:22).

This is the Scriptural manner of telling us that there are five principal temptations that may come to the soul that is striving to build the spiritual temple. The particular form that each temptation takes will vary according to the temperament and circumstances of the subject, but in principle will be the same.

First comes the gold, and this stands for desire for personal power over other people, the desire to regulate their lives, to make them toe the line—our line, naturally—and even to make use of them. Many people on the spiritual path have given way to this temptation. They must dominate other people's souls. They tell themselves that it is done for the good of the victims, of course, but it is really a craving for personal power and glorification. It is not an ignoble sin like that connected with the silver, but for that very reason it is far more dangerous, far-reaching, and enduring.

The thing that gold symbolizes when rightly understood is the omnipresence of God; and of course religious tyranny is a denial of this. You should do all you can to help, to enlighten, and to inspire others, as far as your own understanding will permit, but you must never try to dictate their convictions; or to hold to your own opinions. Religious tyranny is poisonous to the victims; but it is absolutely mortal to the tyrant.

SILVER

Next comes the silver. This stands for greed of money or money's worth, for material objects that can be bought, and even for riches themselves. Or it may be that the offender is not interested in riches themselves but in their ability to give him a position of honor in the eyes of the world. He wants to be considered important and to have adulation or applause. Often he wants to be a "leader," not because he has a message to give but to be important. He is the victim of egotism. Now this is a base and ignoble sin; an insurmountable barrier across the spiritual path.

For the love of money is the root of all evil: which while some coveted after, they have erred from the faith, and pierced themselves through with many sorrows (1 Timothy 6:10).

IVORY, APES, AND PEACOCKS

Then comes the ivory. This stands for undue attachment to a particular teacher, a particular textbook, or a particular church or other organization. It is a mistaken loyalty. It is an unselfish error, but a deadly one. Any religious teacher or writer, however eminent, any church or center, however much beloved, is still but a means to an end. The end itself is spiritual growth.

Recognize with gratitude all the help you receive from any source, but remember that your loyalty is due to God, through your own spiritual development. You must feel free at any time to go wherever you get the most help, irrespective of personal considerations.

The ape stands for bodily temptations such as sensuality, addiction to drink, drugs, and so forth. These things are so obvious that the victim cannot deceive himself about them, so that at least he knows where he stands. They can, of course, be overcome by systematic prayer.

The peacock stands for vanity. Vanity may take the form of intellectual pride, or of a snobbish attitude, or the desire to stand in with what is fashionable and powerful. It also includes spiritual pride on the part of those who really are in Truth, and this is worse than any of the other forms.

But thou, O man of God, flee these things; and follow after righteousness, godliness, faith, love, patience, meekness (1 Timothy 6:11).

Don't try to straddle the fence. If you wish to accomplish anything, you must be single-minded. It will be going the long way around if you first turn left and then right when you really want to go straight ahead. Let nothing turn you from the path. The Bible says,

A double-minded man is unstable in all his ways (James 1:8).

Don't harbor superstitions of any kind, big or little. People often make a fetish of a number or a date, or a keepsake; or they believe certain things bring "bad luck." This is denying God. The Bible says,

Thou shalt have no other gods before me (Exodus 20:3).

Because thou hast made the Lord . . . thy habitation; There shall no evil befall thee . . . (Psalm 91:9–10).

Loosen up. To be tense is the surest way to fail in any undertaking great or small.

To desire success is a splendid thing but to pursue success too tensely is to make certain of missing it. The carefree approach in any endeavor is a shortcut to success. In music, in sport, in study, in business life, many people fail, or advance very slowly, because they make hard work of it.

Treat your work as fun. Regard the difficulties as part of the game, laugh off the annoyances. This, of course, is the real difference between work and play.

Take it easy. *Loosen up!*

For my yoke is easy, and my burden is light (Matthew 11:30).

Change is the law of the universe. Without change, the world would not merely remain in a static state, but it would soon become stale and stagnant. Without change there would be no progress, for change is the essence of betterment. It is obvious that to do anything in a new and better way there must be a change.

Many people look upon change with dread and foreboding. But for those on the spiritual path—for those who believe in God and the power of prayer—change is a fuller expression of life.

When a problem or condition arises in your life that indicates a change, rely upon God, and realize that it is not so much that a door has closed on a chapter of your life, but rather that a door has opened on new and more interesting things.

Behold, I make all things new (Revelation 21:5).

Today most commercial flying is done on a radio beam. A directional beam is produced to guide the pilot to his destination, and as long as he keeps on this beam he knows that he is safe, even if he cannot see around him for fog, or get his bearings in any other way. As soon as he gets off the beam in any direction he is in danger, and he immediately tries to get back on the beam.

Those who believe in the Allness of God, have a spiritual beam upon which to navigate.

You are off the beam the moment you are angry or resentful or jealous or frightened or depressed; and when such a condition arises you should immediately get back on the beam by turning quietly to God in thought, claiming His Presence, claiming that His Love and Intelligence are with you, and that the promises in the Bible are true today. You are back on the beam and you will reach port in safety.

Keep on the beam and nothing shall by any means hurt you.

For this God is our God for ever and ever. He will be our guide even unto death (Psalm 48:14).

I had an amusing experience when I first came to America. Passing an attractive-looking restaurant, I went inside, and selecting a table, sat down and waited. Nothing happened. I continued to wait. All around me, people were enjoying their food, and only I was left out. After a while the truth dawned on me—I was in a cafeteria. (This system had not yet made its appearance in England.) I then realized that while there was plenty of food to be obtained, one had to go forward and claim it for oneself, or go without.

The universe is run exactly on the lines of a cafeteria. Unless you claim—mentally—what you want, you may sit and wait forever.

Ho, every one that thirsteth, come ye to the waters, and he that hath no money; come ye, buy, and eat . . . (Isaiah 55:1).

To me the butterfly teaches the most important lesson that we human beings ever have to learn. You all know his story. He lived what seemed to him a very long time as a worm—what we call the humble caterpillar. Now the life of a caterpillar could be taken as the very type and symbol of restriction. He lives on a green leaf in the forest, and that is about all he knows.

Then one day the little caterpillar finds certain strange stirrings going on within himself. The old green leaf, for some reason, no longer seems sufficient. He becomes moody and discontented, but—and this is the vital point—it is a divine discontent. He feels the need for a bigger, finer, and more interesting life. His instinct tells him that where there is true desire there must be fulfillment.

And so the wonderful thing happens: the butterfly emerges beautiful, graceful, *now endowed with wings,* and instead of crawling about on a restricted leaf, he soars above the trees, above the forest itself—free, unrestricted, his own True Self.

. . . Eye hath not seen, nor ear heard, neither have entered into the heart of man, the things which God hath prepared for them that love him (1 Corinthians 2:9).

What has your religion done for you? For years probably, you have been attending church, reading spiritual books, studying the Bible. Now I suggest that you have a spiritual stocktaking. Ask yourself what difference religion has made in your life, in your home, in your affairs. How much peace of mind has it given you? How much courage? How much understanding? How much opportunity for service? For, make no mistake, real religion does give all these things.

If your spiritual stocktaking does not turn out to be satisfactory, I believe that you will find the explanation to lie in the following law: What you put into your religion, that you get out of it.

If you put in 5 percent of yourself, you will receive a 5 percent dividend or demonstration. If you put in 20 percent of yourself, you will receive a 20 percent demonstration. Complete returns call for a 100 percent investment.

Whatsoever thy hand findeth to do, do it with thy might . . . (Ecclesiastes 9:10).

We often hear the expression "saluting the Christ in him," or "seeing the Christ in him," and we may well ask ourselves what that phrase really means. It is simply the practical application of the rule of Jesus Christ.

Judge not according to the appearance, but judge righteous judgment (John 7:24).

Each of us has a divine Self that is spiritual and perfect but that is never seen on this plane. That is the true man, God's man, and is what we sometimes call "the Christ within." Now whenever you dwell upon or realize the presence of the Christ within yourself or within anyone else, outer appearances begin at once to improve. If somebody displeases you, silently salute the Christ in him. If someone says something against John Smith's character, salute the Christ in him, refuse to discuss the matter, and of course do not repeat it.

The more often you salute the Christ in others, the sooner you will find Him in yourself.

Read Matthew 5:13–16.

In the fifth chapter of Matthew are recorded some of the most powerful pronouncements of Jesus.

Ye are the salt of the earth . . . Ye are the light of the world (Matthew 5:13–14).

It is possible, and, in fact, only too easy, to accept these vital principles as being true; to love the beauty in them; and yet not to put them consistently into practice in one's own life; but this is a perilous attitude, for in that case the salt has lost its savor, and is good for nothing but to be cast out and trodden underfoot.

If you make every effort to practice the teachings of Jesus in every department of your own daily life; if you seek systematically to destroy in yourself selfishness, pride, vanity, sensuality, self-righteousness, jealousy, self-pity, resentment, condemnation, and so forth—not feeding or nourishing them by giving in to them; if you extend the right thought loyally to every person within your ken, then you are worthy to be called *the salt of the earth*.

If you truly live this life, then not only will you make your own demonstration, in the quickest possible time, but you will be, in a very positive sense, a healing and illumining influence on all around you. You will be a blessing to men and women in remote places and times, men and women of whom you have never heard, and who will never hear of you—*a light of the world*.

Let your light so shine before men, that they may see your good works, and glorify your Father which is in heaven (Matthew 5:16).

The state of your soul is always expressed in your outer conditions and in the intangible influence that you radiate at large. There is a cosmic law that nothing can permanently deny its own nature. Emerson said: "What you are shouts so loudly that I cannot hear what you say." The soul that is built upon prayer cannot be hidden, it shines out brightly through the life that it lives. It speaks for itself, but in utter silence, and does much of its best work unconsciously. Its mere presence heals and blesses all around it.

And I, *if I be lifted up from the earth, will draw all men unto me* (John 12:32).

Never try to force other people to accept spiritual truth. Instead, see to it that they are so favorably impressed by your own life and conduct, and by the peace and joy that radiate from you, that they will come running to you of their own accord, begging you to give them the wonderful thing that you have. To do this is to make your soul truly *the city upon a hill that cannot be hidden* because it is the City of God. This is to *let your light shine* to the glorifying of your Father which is in Heaven.

Read Matthew 5:17–20.

If anyone were so insane as to suppose that the knowledge of the Truth of Being could put him "above" the moral law, in the sense of authorizing him to break it, he would speedily discover that he had made a tragic mistake. The more spiritual knowledge that one possesses, the more severe is the punishment which one brings upon oneself by any infraction of the moral law. The Christian has to be very much more careful than other people. Indeed, all real spiritual understanding must necessarily be accompanied by definite moral improvement. A theoretical acceptance of the letter of Truth might go with moral carelessness (greatly to the peril of the delinquent), but it is impossible to make any real spiritual progress unless you are trying your very best to live the life. It is impossible to divorce true spiritual knowledge from right conduct.

For I say unto you, That except your righteousness shall exceed the righteousness of the scribes and Pharisees, ye shall in no case enter into the kingdom of heaven (Matthew 5:20).

Think not that I am come to destroy the law, or the prophets: I am not come to destroy, but to fulfill.

For verily I say unto you, Till heaven and earth pass, one jot or one tittle shall in no wise pass from the law, till all be fulfilled (Matthew 5:17–18).

A "jot" or yod was the smallest letter in the Hebrew alphabet, like the Greek "iota." A "tittle" (really "little horn") is one of those tiny spurs or projections that distinguish certain Hebrew letters.

The scribes and the Pharisees were for the most part worthy men leading strictly moral lives according to appearances. Their faults were the weaknesses of the religious formalist everywhere—spiritual pride and self-righteousness. Of these faults they were unconscious—that is the deadly malice of these diseases of the soul—but they did strive to fulfill the law as they understood it. Jesus knew this, and he gave them credit for it. Here he warns his followers that unless their practical conduct is better than that of these people, they need not suppose that they are engaged on the spiritual path.

As you grow in spiritual power and understanding you will find that many outer regulations will become unnecessary; but this will be because you have really risen above them. This point in your development, where your understanding of Truth enables you to dispense with certain outer props and regulations, is the spiritual coming of age.

However, this spiritual coming of age cannot be hurried or forced, but must appear when the consciousness is ready, exactly as the flowering of a bulb can only be the result of natural growth. You have to demonstrate where you are. To seek to demonstrate beyond your understanding is not spiritual. Fix your attention upon spiritual things, and without consciously trying to make haste you will be amazed to discover the pace at which your soul has hastened.

To take a simple example: Suppose that in a street accident you find that a man has severed an artery and the blood is spurting out. The normal course is that unless this bleeding is stopped the victim will die. Now, what is the spiritual attitude to take in such a case? Claim the ability of God to heal. If your faith is strong enough the severed artery will immediately be healed. But if your faith fails, you must take the usual steps to save the man's life by immediately improvising a tourniquet, or whatever the proper procedure may be, still claiming divine aid.

Let us hold fast the profession of our faith without wavering; (for he is faithful that promised) . . . (Hebrews 10:23).

What of the man who is conscious of considerable moral imperfection, perhaps of the habit of grave sin, and is at the same time sincerely desirous of spiritual growth? Is he to relinquish the quest for spiritual knowledge until he has first reformed his conduct? By no means. As a matter of fact any attempt to improve himself morally without spiritual aid is foredoomed to failure. The thing to do is to pray regularly and to throw the responsibility for success upon God. The man must carry on, no matter how many times he may fail. Let him keep affirming that God is helping him, and that his own real nature is spiritual and perfect. In this way moral regeneration and spiritual unfoldment will go hand in hand. The Christian life does not require that we possess perfection of character, or else, which of us would be able to live it? What it does require is honest, genuine striving for that perfection.

    . . . he that is perfect in knowledge is with thee (Job 36:4).

Y*e have heard that it was said by them of old time, Thou shalt not kill; and whosoever shall kill shall be in danger of the judgment:*

But I say unto you, That whosoever is angry with his brother without a cause shall be in danger of the judgment: and whosoever shall say to his brother, Raca, shall be in danger of the council; but whosoever shall say, Thou fool, shall be in danger of hell fire (Matthew 5:21–22).

The Old Law said "Thou shalt not kill," but Jesus says that even to want to kill, nay, even to be angry with your brother, is sufficient to keep you out of the Kingdom of Heaven. It was a distinct gain when primitive people could be persuaded not to murder but to develop sufficient self-control to master their anger. Spiritual demonstration demands that anger itself be overcome. It is simply not possible to get any experience of God worth talking about, or to exercise spiritual power until you have gotten rid of resentment and condemnation. You can have either your demonstration or your indignation, but you cannot have both.

Therefore if thou bring thy gift to the altar, and there rememberest that thy brother hath aught against thee;

Leave there thy gift before the altar, and go thy way; first be reconciled to thy brother, and then come and offer thy gift (Matthew 5:23–24).

Indignation, resentment, the desire to punish other people, the desire to "get even," the feeling "it serves him right"; all these things form a quite impenetrable barrier to spiritual power. Jesus says that if you are bringing a gift to the altar, and you remember that your brother has anything against you, you must put down your gift and go make peace with your brother; when you have done that, your offering will be acceptable.

Jesus builds up this tremendous lesson in the Oriental tradition. He says first that whoever is angry with his brother shall be in danger; second that to be hostile to another, is to be in grave danger; and finally that to hold so low an opinion about a fellow creature as to consider him outside the pale, is to shut ourselves off from any hope of spiritual fruit while we remain in this state of mind.

Note carefully that the King James version of the Bible here makes a serious error, which has been corrected in the revised version. It interpolates a phrase not in the earliest manuscripts and makes Jesus say, "Whosoever is angry without a cause"; which is a manifest absurdity. No sane person gets angry without what he deems to be a cause. What Jesus said was that whoever is angry with his brother under any circumstances is in danger.

116

Agree with thine adversary quickly, whiles thou art in the way with him; lest at any time the adversary deliver thee to the judge, and the judge deliver thee to the officer, and thou be cast into prison.

Verily I say unto thee, Thou shalt by no means come out thence, till thou hast paid the uttermost farthing (Matthew 5:25–26).

Jesus is stressing here the instruction contained in his injunction to "watch and pray." It is ever so much easier to overcome a difficulty if you tackle it at its first appearance than it will be after the trouble has had time to establish itself in your mentality—to dig itself in, as the soldiers say. The moment a difficulty presents itself to your attention, quietly affirm the Truth, giving it no chance to dig itself in.

On the other hand, by thinking about your difficulty, you incorporate it into your mentality, and if you go on doing this long enough, it may be exceedingly difficult to get rid of it.

Jesus, when he wished to drive home a particularly important point, employed a graphic illustration from everyday life. In those times the law governing debtors was extremely severe. When a man found himself in debt, it behooved him to come to terms with his creditor as quickly as possible. Even at the present day it is important for the debtor to keep his case from coming into court, for the longer the case drags on the more do lawyers' fees, court dues, and expenses of various kinds accumulate, all piled on top of the debt proper. So it is with the various difficulties that present themselves to us in our daily lives.

By coming to terms with the adversary in the first place, that is to say, by getting our thought right immediately concerning any difficulty, we incur no "costs" and the transaction remains a simple one.

Suppose that you find yourself sneezing. If you say: "There, now, I have caught cold again; I am in for it!" and then proceed to dwell upon the thought that you have caught cold, you are giving the trouble the opportunity to dig itself in to your mentality. People often indulge in quite a meditation upon colds. Instead, if at the first moment that the possibility of catching cold occurs to you, you immediately reject it and affirm the Truth, the whole thing will be over in a short time.

Or perhaps upon opening your morning mail you find a notice informing you that your bank has failed. Many people in such a case would saturate themselves with the thought of ruin by rehearsing every kind of difficulty that might come. However, the proper thing to do, immediately upon becoming aware of the news, is to turn to God—your real support—and refuse to accept the suggestion of trouble as binding; literally drive the thought of loss, fear, and resentment out of consciousness. If you do this, working steadily until peace of mind is restored, you will presently find that in some way or other the trouble will disappear. Either the bank will speedily recover itself—and there is no reason at all why one person's prayer should not save the bank and the fortunes of thousands—or, if this is not possible, you will find your loss equalized in some other way.

. . . *whosoever shall call upon the name of the Lord shall be saved* (Romans 10:13).

Ye have heard that it was said by them of old time, Thou shalt not commit adultery:

But I say unto you, That whosoever looketh on a woman to lust after her hath committed adultery with her already in his heart (Matthew 5:27–28).

In this unforgettable paragraph, Jesus stresses the master truth, so utterly fundamental, yet so unsuspected by the world at large, that what really matters is thought. People have always been accustomed to suppose that as long as their deeds conformed to the law, they have done all that can be reasonably expected of them, and that their thoughts and feelings are their own business. But the type of thought that we allow to become habitual will sooner or later find expression on the plane of action.

The logical consequence of this fact is very startling. It means that if you entertain covetous thoughts for your neighbor's money, you are a thief, even though you may not yet have put your hand in the till. The adulterer at heart is corrupting his soul even though his impure thought is never expressed on the physical plane. Lust, jealousy, vengeance, mentally entertained, carry the soul's consent, and this soul-consent is the malice of sin.

Keep thy heart with all diligence, for out of it are the issues of life (Proverbs 4:23).

And *if thy right eye offend thee, pluck it out, and cast it from thee: for it is profitable for thee that one of thy members should perish, and not that thy whole body should be cast into hell.*

And if thy right hand offend thee, cut it off, and cast it from thee: for it is profitable for thee that one of thy members should perish, and not that thy whole body should be cast into hell (Matthew 5:29–30).

The soul's integrity is the one and only thing that matters. And so Jesus insists that positively no sacrifice can be too great to insure the integrity of one's soul. Anything that stands in the way of that, must be given up.

Whatever is standing between us and our true contact with God—a sin, an old grudge left unforgiven, stark greed for the things of this world—must go. Such things, however, are so obvious that at least the transgressor is aware of them; it is the subtle things like self-love, self-righteousness, and spiritual pride, that are most difficult for the self to exercise.

It hath been said, Whosoever shall put away his wife, let him give her a miting of divorcement:

But I say unto you, That whosoever shall put away his wife, saving for the cause of fornication, causeth her to commit adultery: and whosoever shall marry her that is divorced committeth adultery (Matthew 5:31–32).

We are told that in those days divorces were granted by the rabbinical law on the most trifling grounds. Married people who were not getting on together as well as they would have liked, were prone to run away from that problem by obtaining an easy dissolution. Now we understand that no permanent happiness can be obtained in this way. As long as you are running away from your problem, you will continue to meet it in a new guise at every turn in the road.

Just as in running from one business position to another, without first having brought about a change in consciousness, we find ourselves but repeating the old conditions in a slightly different form, so, as a rule, people who divorce freely are apt to finish up as dissatisfied as they began. The general rule in Truth is, fight out your problem where you are, with prayer.

The general rule is still good for all conditions in life: Do not try to divorce or amputate the inharmony, but let it dissolve away of itself under God's guidance.

Read Matthew 5:33–37.

Again, ye have heard that it hath been said by them of old time, Thou shalt not forswear thyself, but shalt perform unto the Lord thine oaths:

But let your communication be, Yea, yea; Nay, nay: for whatsoever is more than these cometh of evil (Matthew 5:33, 37).

Swear not at all, is one of the cardinal points in the teaching of Jesus. It means, briefly, that you are not to mortgage your future conduct in advance; to seek to fix your conduct or your belief for tomorrow while it is yet today. Rather you are constantly to keep yourself an open channel for the pouring out of the Holy Spirit into manifestation through you.

Of course, Jesus does not mean that you are not to enter into ordinary business engagements. Nor does he mean that the ordinary oath administered in a court of law is inadmissible. These things are matters of legal convenience. The Sermon on the Mount is a treatise on the spiritual life, for the spiritual life controls all the rest.

Read Matthew 5:38–42.

But I say unto you, That ye resist not evil . . . (Matthew 5:39).

Jesus is a revolutionary teacher. He turns the world upside down for those who accept his teaching. When once you have accepted the Jesus Christ message, all values change radically.

The old law was that whatever man did to man, he should himself be made to suffer by way of punishment. If he put out another man's eye, his own was put out by the officers of justice; if he killed, he was killed.

The desire to "get even," to get one's own back, to level things up somehow or other, when we have been hurt or have suffered injustice, or witnessed things of which we did not approve, will remain with us until the time when we definitely take ourselves in hand and destroy it. "Revenge," said Bacon, "is a kind of wild justice."

Now Jesus reverses this and says that when someone injures you, you are to forgive him. No matter what the provocation may be, and no matter how many times it is repeated, you are to loose him and let him go, for thus only can you be freed yourself.

"Hatred ceases not with hatred," said the Light of Asia, enunciating this great cosmic truth many centuries earlier, and the Light of the World put it in the forefront of his teaching because it is the cornerstone of man's salvation.

This doctrine of "resist not evil" is the great metaphysical secret. To the world it sounds like moral suicide, the feeblest surrender to aggression; but in the light of the Jesus Christ revelation it is seen to be superb spiritual strategy. Antagonize any situation, and you give it power against yourself; offer mental nonresistance, and it crumbles away in front of you.

Jesus gives no instructions for details of external conduct, and so the references here to suing at law, to coat and cloak, to lending and borrowing, to turning the other cheek, are illustrative and symbolical of mental states, and are not to be taken in the narrow literal sense. We cannot too often remind ourselves that if the thought is right, the deed cannot be wrong. No teacher could ever say that a given act must necessarily be right at any time, because the play of circumstances in human life is too hopelessly complicated for any such prediction.

If, when someone is behaving badly, you will immediately switch your attention from the human to the Divine, and concentrate upon God, or upon the real spiritual self of the person in question, you will find that his conduct will immediately change. This is the true revenge.

Dearly beloved, avenge not yourselves . . . for it is written, Vengeance is mine; I will repay, saith the Lord (Romans 12:19).

If somebody comes into the room at home, or into the office or shop, looking as if he meant to make trouble, just try switching your attention straight to the Divine, instead of squaring up aggressively to meet the difficulty or shrinking away to avoid it, according to your temperament. You will be amused and gratified to see the anger fade from the subject's face (which will mean that it has faded from his heart too) and quite a different expression take its place.

I have myself seen several cases where men, and on two occasions, children, were actually fighting, and upon a spectator's "turning the check" the strife ceased like magic. Animals respond even more easily to this treatment than do human beings. I have seen two instances where dogs were fighting savagely and all efforts to separate them had failed, when the realization of the Presence of God's love in all His creatures restored peace. In one case it took several minutes' work; in the other it was practically instantaneous.

Be not overcome of evil, but overcome evil with good (Romans 12:21).

Read Matthew 5:43–47.

But I say unto you, Love your enemies, bless them that curse you, do good to them that hate you, and pray for them which despitefully use you, and persecute you; That ye may be the children of your Father which is in heaven . . . (Matthew 5:44–45).

Right reaction is the supreme art of life, and Jesus compressed the secret of that art into a sentence when he said: *Resist not evil.* A correct understanding of this commandment will regenerate your body, liberate your soul, and remake your life.

Love is God and is therefore absolutely all-powerful. Meeting hatred with Love is the perfect method of self-defense in all circumstances. It renders you absolutely invulnerable to any kind of attack.

If you receive bad news, if you are unhappy in your work, or in your home, feel out mentally for the Presence of divine Spirit, all around you; affirm its actuality; and claim that God has dominion over all conditions, and you will soon be free.

And this commandment have we from him, That he who loveth God love his brother also (1 John 4:21).

Be ye therefore perfect, even as your Father which is in heaven is perfect (Matthew 5:48).

Consider carefully what Jesus is saying. He is commanding us to be perfect, even as God Himself is perfect; and, as we know that Jesus will not command the impossible, he has here given his authority to the doctrine that it is possible for man to become divinely perfect. And, more than this, he is putting it forward as a thing that will have to be actually done.

Now, if we really are the children of God, capable of eternal and flawless perfection, there can be no real power in evil, not even in sin, to keep us permanently in bondage. So now let us lose no further time before commencing our upward march. Let us now—at this very moment, if we have not already done so—rise up, like the prodigal son amid the husks of materiality and limitation, and cry, with all confidence in the teachings and promises of Jesus:

I will arise and go to my father (Luke 15:18).

When you fight a thing you antagonize it and it hits back. The harder you fight it the harder it hits. When you give your attention to anything, you are building that thing into your consciousness, for good or evil.

A story is told about William Penn. He had been accustomed from boyhood to carrying a sword because it was part of the dress of a gentleman at that period. One day it occurred to him that this was inconsistent with his Quakerism; but on the other hand he knew that he would feel extremely embarrassed without it. So he consulted George Fox, never doubting that his leader would say, "You must stop wearing it." George Fox was silent for a few moments, and then said, "Carry thy sword until thou canst no longer carry it."

A year or so later Penn discontinued the practice quite easily.

When you are faced with some negative condition, withdraw your attention from it by building the opposite into your subconscious. Then the undesirable thing falls away like an overripe fruit.

Finally, brethren, whatsoever things are true, whatsoever things are honest, whatsoever things are just, whatsoever things are pure, whatsoever things are lovely, whatsoever things are of good report; if there be any virtue, and if there be any praise, think on these things (Philippians 4:8).

Prayer does change things. Let us be perfectly clear about this. *Prayer does change things*. Many people say that prayer is a good thing because it gives us courage and fortitude for meeting our troubles. They say that prayer often gets a man out of difficulty simply by giving him self-confidence that he would otherwise have lacked. Of course, this is not spiritual Truth. The fact is that seeing the Presence of God where the trouble seems to be does not merely give us courage to meet the trouble; it changes the trouble into harmony.

Prayer heals the body by changing the tissues, and it does this by first changing the mind that forms them. Prayer brings man his salvation by changing his nature fundamentally; not by making the best of him as he is. The body, the environment, the universe itself, is plastic to our thought; and it always reflects our sincere belief.

For as he thinketh in his heart, so is he (Proverbs 23:7).

Those who are perplexed by the difficulties and seeming inconsistencies of life should remember that at the present time we get only a partial view of things; and that a partial view of anything never shows the thing as it really is. If you were to show an Eskimo any number of pictures of sections of a horse, but never a picture of the whole horse, he would never know what the animal really looked like.

So it is with life. Some day (when we have enough spiritual growth) we will come to see that the seemingly disjointed happenings, the apparent accidents, are really part of an orderly pattern.

Judge not according to the appearance, but judge righteous judgment (John 7:24).

Many people would like to attend what they call an advanced class in metaphysics; but what could an advanced course include that would not be in the ordinary lessons?

The usual metaphysical classes teach that God is the only power, and that evil is insubstantial; that we form our own destiny by our thoughts and our beliefs; that conditions do not matter when we pray; that time and space and matter are human illusions; that there is a solution to every problem; that man is the child of God, and God is perfect good; that Jesus Christ is the one who taught the full truth about God, and actually demonstrated it.

Once the student has obtained a correct intellectual comprehension of these facts, and digested them—at least partially—the only thing that remains for him is to develop his understanding by demonstrating them in practice.

So we see that the real advanced course is the one we give ourselves by demonstrating over the practical problems of everyday life.

Faith without works is dead (James 2:20).

We live in the Presence of God. The Bible says, *In him we live, and move, and have our being* (Acts 17:28). This limitless Power, which is Intelligence and Love—God—can be contacted at any time by turning to Him in thought, and allowing Him to fill our hearts. Whenever we do this He at once begins to influence our lives for peace and harmony and freedom.

A party of shipwrecked sailors were drifting in an open boat on the Atlantic Ocean. They had no water, and were suffering agonies from thirst. Another small boat came within hailing distance, and when the shipwrecked mariners cried out for water, the newcomers said, "let down your bucket." This sounded like cruel mockery. But when the advice was repeated several times, one of the sailors dipped the bucket overboard—and drew up clean, fresh, sparkling water!

For several days they had been sailing through fresh water and did not know it. They were out of sight of land, but off the estuary of the Amazon, which carries fresh water many miles out to sea.

Closer is he than breathing; nearer than hands and feet.—Tennyson

Jesus said, *It is easier for a camel to go through the eye of a needle, than for a rich man to enter the kingdom of God* (Mark 10:25).

The simile used by Jesus was a graphic one for his listeners. In those days every important city was surrounded by a wall for defense. There would be a large gate in the wall and this would be closed at sunset and placed under an armed guard. There was usually, however, a low wicket gate known as the needle's eye, set in the big door. When a laden camel arrived after sunset the only way it could get in was to be unloaded of all merchandise, whereupon it would squirm on its knees through the needle's eye.

Unload your camel if you want to enter the Kingdom of Heaven. You do this, of course, not by getting rid of conditions in themselves, but by getting rid of your sense of dependency on them. Very often you will find yourself so glad to be without a lot of that merchandise that you will never put it back.

People often say that when they first came to the knowledge of truth it seemed that miracles happened almost every day. Negative conditions of long standing disappeared. Then, they say, a sort of slump seemed to set in, since which they have never been able to do so well.

Now why should this be the case? The explanation is that what demonstrates is an expansion of consciousness. With an expansion of consciousness our conditions must improve. When people first learn of the omnipresence of God, they experience such an expansion. Then the tendency is to rest upon the first knowledge acquired, and to make their early realization serve over and over again. This will not do. It is only today's realization that will demonstrate, never yesterday's or last year's.

God is not the God of the dead, but of the living (Matthew 22:32).

God is infinite perfection and he is not concerned with our limited ideas about time and space and matter.

For thus saith the high and lofty One that inhabiteth eternity, whose name is Holy; I dwell in the high and holy place, with him also that is of a contrite and humble spirit, to revive the spirit of the humble, and to revive the heart of the contrite ones (Isaiah 57:15).

God is not progressing or improving. What improves is our understanding of Him, and as this happens all our conditions necessarily improve too. There never was a time in your history when God was not all that He is today, and there never can come a time when God will be any more than He is today.

God is continually expressing Himself in new ways—but this is not improvement; it is unfoldment. Your life is simply part of this unfoldment, and that is the only reason for your existing at all. You are the living expression of God now—and to understand this is salvation.

One philosopher has defined life as adaptation to environment. He said that anything that was alive would try to survive by adapting itself to the conditions in which it had to live. There is of course a great deal of truth in this view. Life is tenacious and extraordinarily resourceful in fitting itself to unsuitable conditions.

When we come to humanity, however, the Bible teaches us that man does not have to adapt himself to outer conditions but that he has the power of changing or adapting outer things to fit him. This is the vital distinction between materialism and spiritual Truth. You have within you the divine Spark—the Indwelling Christ—and by awakening and developing this, your spiritual nature, you can mold conditions to fit your needs.

Man has free will, the power of reason and intuition. By learning to use these faculties he gains his dominion. It is the Bible that says that God has given man dominion over all things.

The Lord will give strength unto his people . . . (Psalm 29:11).

The royal road to progress in spiritual understanding is to solve *definite* problems by prayer.

Every time that you heal any condition, however small, by prayer, you gain an increase in spiritual understanding. One definite healing will teach you more about spiritual truth than hours of discussion or reading.

Some questions in metaphysics that readily present themselves cannot be answered without a good deal of preparation, and it is useless to try to answer them until this ground has been covered. It is useless for a student of algebra to try to understand binomial theorem if he hardly understands a simple equation. You always have enough understanding to get freedom and harmony here and now in the place where you are.

Because thou hast asked . . . for thyself understanding to discern judgment . . . lo, I have given thee a wise and an understanding heart . . . (1 Kings 3:11–12).

Never hesitate to approach God in prayer because you are not worthy. If we had to wait until we were worthy, no one would ever find salvation, because we cannot make ourselves worthy. Turn to God, just as you are, and, however sinful you may feel yourself to be, God will begin to make you worthy, as long as your turning to him is wholehearted.

Only God can cancel mistakes and rebuild our lives. The more sense of guilt we may have the more reason is there for turning to Him. The very fact that you are praying means that God Himself has initiated the prayer, and what thought can be greater than this?

Ho, every one that thirsteth, come ye to the waters, and he that hath no money; come ye, buy and eat . . . (Isaiah 55:1).

Your present problem is your great opportunity. Your own mind—the Secret Place, as Jesus called it—is the council chamber where the arrangements and decisions for your whole life are made; it is also the drafting room where the plans for your destiny are formed. Your life is your laboratory. The world is your workshop.

The reason that you are here is that you may develop spiritually; and the way to do that is to meet the challenge of practical life. You do not develop spiritually by running away from life into some sheltered retreat. Nor do you grow in spiritual stature by gaining your point through will power.

It is the law that any difficulties that can come to you at any time, must be exactly what you need most at the moment to enable you to take the next step forward by overcoming them. The only real misfortune, the only real tragedy, comes when we suffer without learning the lesson.

I pray not that thou shouldst take them out of the world, but that thou shouldst keep them from the evil (John 17:15).

139

Really there are only two feelings that a human being can have, namely love and fear. It is generally supposed that the kinds of feeling we may have are legion, but this is an illusion. All other feelings, so-called, will turn out upon analysis to be either love or fear.

What about anger? Well, anger is really but fear in disguise. In chemistry we occasionally find the same substance occurring under completely different appearances. For example, black lead is exactly the same substance chemically as a diamond, different as they look. They are said to be allotropic forms of carbon. In the same way, anger, hatred, jealousy, criticism, egotism, are but allotropic forms of fear.

Joy, interest, the feeling of success and accomplishment, the appreciation of art, are allotropic forms of love. The great difference between the two feelings is that love is always creative, and fear is always destructive. It is for us to decide which of these two feelings shall hold sway in our lives.

God is love; and he that dwelleth in love dwelleth in God, and God in Him (1 John 4:16).

But thou, when thou prayest, enter into thy closet, and when thou hast shut thy door, pray to thy Father which is in secret; and thy Father which seeth in secret shall reward thee openly.

But when ye pray, use not vain repetitions, as the heathen do: for they think that they shall be heard for their much speaking (Matthew 6:6–7).

The sixth chapter of Matthew presents the doctrine of the Secret Place and its importance as the controlling center of the "Kingdom." It is the essential factor of the teaching of Jesus Christ. You are a king, Jesus says, the ruler of your own kingdom. When you know the truth of being, you are the absolute monarch of your own life.

It is very significant that Jesus should call your consciousness the Secret Place. It is obvious that nothing has any real significance but a change of policy in the Secret Place.

A distinguished Quaker some years ago said: "In my youth we discontinued the distinctive Quaker costume and certain other usages because we realized that people who were far from really caring for our Quaker ideals were joining us, nevertheless, for the sake of the educational facilities they could obtain so inexpensively for their children, as well as other advantages of our membership. It was so easy to style oneself a 'Friend,' to purchase and wear a coat without buttons or collar, and to interlard the conversation with a grammatical peculiarity, while leaving the character completely untouched. It is so easy to buy and wear ceremonial garments, to repeat set prayers by rote at certain times, to use stereotyped forms of devotion, to attend religious services at prescribed periods—and to leave the heart unchanged."

It is unquestionable that the spiritualization of thought does un-doubtedly lead the student to simplify his mode of life, for so many things that previously seemed important are now found to be unimportant and uninteresting. It is unquestionable too, that he gradually finds himself meeting different people, reading different books, spending his time differently; and that his conversation naturally changes its quality. These things follow upon the change of heart; never can they precede it.

. . . *old things are passed away, behold, all things are become new* (2 Corinthians 5:17).

Now we see how vain is the foolish attempt to cultivate the good opinion of other people under the impression that such a thing can be of any real advantage to us. Jesus has exposed that kind of fallacy once and for all. He says that the applause that follows upon outer acts is the only reward they ever bring, and that results worth while are only to be obtained in the Secret Place of consciousness.

. . . *pray to thy Father which is in secret; and thy Father which seeth in secret shall reward thee openly* (Matthew 6:6).

M oreover *when ye fast, be not, as the hypocrites, of a sad counte-
nance for they disfigure their faces, that they may appear unto men to fast.
Verily I say unto you, They have their reward.*

*But thou, when thou fastest, anoint thine head, and wash thy face;
That thou appear not unto men to fast, but unto thy Father which is in se-
cret and thy Father, which seeth in secret, shall reward thee openly*
(Matthew 6:16–18).

Jesus takes the practice of fasting for granted. Now the most profitable method of fasting is abstention from negative or error thoughts.
In some cases it is necessary to abstain for a time from thinking about
a particular problem at all. There are certain problems, usually those
that you have been mulling over too much, that are overcome "only
by prayer and fasting." In such a case it is best to give the problem a
definite and final prayer, and then to leave it alone, for a time; or
else hand it over bodily to someone else to handle for you, after which
you keep your thoughts completely away from it.

Read Matthew 6:16–23.

If your consciousness is right, that is, if you have a good under-standing of God as the loving Source of your boundless supply, you will always be able to demonstrate whatever money or goods you may require. You cannot want for anything when once you truly realize that in divine Mind demand and supply are one. And, on the con-trary, until you do realize this, you never will be really safe from want.

In the long run, no one can retain what does not belong to him by right of consciousness, nor be deprived of that which is truly his by the same supreme title.

If you are looking to outer, passing, mutable things for either happiness or security, you are not putting God first. If you are putting God first in your life, you will not find yourself laboring under undue anxiety about anything, *for where your treasure is, there will your heart be also* (Matthew 6:21).

If you pray for yourself in the right way every day, you will find that the minor things of life will gradually fall correctly into place of their own accord without any trouble on your part. Contrast this with the usual method of trying to get everything right by separately organizing a thousand petty details, and you will appreciate how wonderfully the new spiritual basis sets you free. *If therefore thine eye be single, thy whole body shall be full of light* (Matthew 6:22).

The eye symbolizes spiritual perception. *Whatever you give your attention to, is the thing that governs your life.* Attention is the key. Your free will lies in the directing of your attention. Whatever you steadfastly direct your attention to, will come into your life and dominate it. If you do not direct your attention consistently to anything in particular—and many people do not—then nothing in particular will come into your life except uncertainty and suspense.

If the Glory of God comes first with you, and to express His Will becomes the rule of your life, then your eye is single and your whole body, or embodiment, will be full of light.

Read Matthew 6:24–33.

Many Christians accept these facts theoretically, but are less than halfhearted when it comes to their practical application, and this vacillation lands them in difficulties that always follow upon inconsistency and weakness. To try to rest sometimes upon the material basis, and sometimes upon the spiritual, is to try to serve two masters, and this of course cannot be done. *Ye cannot serve God and mammon* (Matthew 6:24).

Man is essentially spiritual, the image and likeness of God, and therefore he is made for the spiritual basis, and he cannot really succeed on any other.

Read Matthew 6:25–35.

Wherefore, if God so clothe the grass of the field . . . shall he not much more clothe you, O ye of little faith? (Matthew 6:30).

Of course, Jesus did not mean that you as a human being are to copy the lives or the methods of the birds or flowers literally, for you are infinitely higher in the scale of creation than they are. The lesson is that you are to adapt yourself as completely to your element as they do to theirs. Your true element is the Presence of God. When man accepts the Truth that in God he lives and moves and has his being, as completely and unquestioningly as the birds and the flowers accept the truth of their condition, he will demonstrate as easily and as thoroughly as they do.

One hears occasionally of curious cases of people who claim to be so spiritual that they do not feel called upon to earn their own living. Someone else who is not too spiritual to go to work, is expected to keep them. But this attitude of mind speaks for itself. If your understanding is sufficient to enable you to dispense with ordinary work, you will find yourself automatically supplied in an independent and self-respecting manner—with a good living. This cannot possibly apply to people who are in debt or sponging upon others. If you really wish to try the experiment of "stepping out" upon the power of the Word, be sure that your so doing is authentic. The only way to make this experiment in a genuine manner is to let it be "demonstrate or starve." If you are secretly looking to someone else to come to the rescue, you are not really depending upon the Word.

Take therefore no thought for the morrow for the morrow shall take thought for the things of itself. Sufficient unto the day is the evil thereof (Matthew 6:34).

Always remember that the only thought that you need to concern yourself with is the present time. The thoughts of yesterday or of last year do not matter now, because if you can get the present thought right it will make everything else right here and now. The best way to prepare for tomorrow is to make today's consciousness serene and harmonious.

Never go delving in your mind to look for troubles to pray about. Deal faithfully with those that bring themselves to your attention, and hidden things will be taken care of.

Have faith in your own faith. Have faith enough in yourself to believe that you really have enough faith to move mountains. Is this a strange idea? Probably it is for many people, yet Jesus taught it.

People are constantly saying that they wish they had more faith because if they had they could get better results. You have to realize, however, that this attitude of mind is extremely negative. It is affirming, although indirectly, that your faith is very poor—and you know what that means.

Jesus said that the very smallest amount of faith (like a grain of mustard seed) is sufficient. If you have faith enough to pray at all, you have enough faith to start with. If you had no faith, you would not be praying.

Have faith in your own faith, and that in itself will build it up more and more until the work is done.

. . . *be not faithless, but believing* (John 20:27).

Everyone on the spiritual path has found that it happens occasionally in the early years—and not often then—that he suddenly finds himself almost or quite unable to pray. Often it seems that he cannot get any sense of contact with God. This naturally depresses him and sometimes leads to greater fear and almost to despair.

Now, these severe reactions are not necessary, once you know that everyone goes through them.

This trouble is caused by overdoing. You have been praying too long or too hard, or you have been giving too much time to spiritual work exclusively, instead of having other interests in your life too. It is really a condition of staleness and psychological congestion. The medieval mystics called these times "seasons of dryness" and suffered severely because they believed them to be sinful.

The remedy is not to struggle, but to know that this dryness will surely pass, and your spiritual joy return. If you cannot pray, do not try, but think, "God is so good that I need not pray; he will take care of me anyway." (Of course, this itself is a wonderful prayer.) On a long motor tour, it sometimes happens that you come upon a piece of rough, bad road. For hundreds of miles the going has been perfect, but now you are shaken and bumped badly, but you do not worry, because you know for certain that it will only last for a few miles. Indeed, there is probably a notice saying "Pavement ahead."

. . . *weeping may endure for a night, but joy cometh in the morning* (Psalm 30:5).

When Nebuchadnezzar sent out his decree that everyone in his kingdom should bow down and worship the golden image that he had erected, there were three men who refused to obey. These were Shadrach, Meshach, and Abed-nego, Hebrew officials in the province of Babylon.

Nebuchadnezzar called them before him, and they bluntly told the King that their God would deliver them from the fiery furnace to which they would be consigned, but even if God did not deliver them, they would still serve Him and Him alone.

Nebuchadnezzar had the three men thrust into the fiery furnace, and the heat was so intense that it slew the guards who threw them in. Then, as he looked in upon the three faithful Hebrews, Nebuchadnezzar was astonished to find a *fourth man* walking in the flames with the other three. Shadrach, Meshach, and Abed-nego walked out of the fiery furnace without blemish or scar.

So it is when we hold steadfastly to God, and give all power to Him. He sends his messenger to deliver us from our furnace of fear and frustration. Then do we know that nothing shall by any means harm us.

Blessed be the God of Shadrach, Meshach, and Abed-nego, who hath sent his angel, and delivered his servants that trusted in him . . . (Daniel 3:28).

*F*or he is our peace, who hath made both one, and hath broken down the middle wall or partition between us *(Ephesians 2:14).*

This is not only one of the most beautiful texts in the Bible, but one of the most important. Consider what it says. First, that God is our peace; next, that not only are we and God one (all spiritual teachers say that) but that it is He who has made us one. We are one because that is the nature of being since He has made us that way. Then the inspired writer uses a figure of speech. He reminds us that when we lost our sense of unity with God, it is exactly as though a wall was built between God and ourselves. When that happens communication is broken and we are no longer one in consciousness, until, of course, the wall is pulled down.

In any difficulty the one important thing is to have the temporary wall of partition pulled down, and to let God do it—for only He can.

We all know that it is God alone who is our peace—although nearly all of us tend to forget it from time to time. We forget it when we begin to neglect our daily visit with God.

Now, when you think that you are too busy for your daily visit, let me ask you frankly, what wonderful thing are you doing that is more important? There is nothing that you could possibly do with that time that would bring you greater benefit than perfect peace. As a matter of fact, if you have something very important and urgent to do, your visit will make that very important thing go through much more easily and successfully.

Acquaint now thyself with him, and be at peace . . . (Job 22:21).

People are to be judged by their actions. We sometimes hear it said, "His conduct is bad but at heart he means well"; but this is nonsense. In the old-fashioned phrase, "handsome is as handsome does."

The bad-tempered person cannot possibly have "a heart of gold" as is sometimes charitably said. A bad-tempered person has a mean, selfish heart and should get busy and change it without delay.

One who loves does not seek his own advantage. Love acts the part, and anything else is hypocrisy.

. . . *be ye kind one to another, tenderhearted, forgiving one another, even as God for Christ's sake hath forgiven you* (Ephesians 4:32).

People are very apt to find what they seek. You have noticed that people who go about looking for trouble, practically always find it. The popular proverb, "Listeners seldom hear good of themselves," is an example. We also know people who love to say that they never have any luck. When things seem to go against them, they exclaim triumphantly, "Wouldn't you know it?—that is what always happens to me!"

Now, such a mistaken person needs only to alter this habit and he will automatically alter his life. It is often difficult to get such people to make this alteration, but if they do the result is never in doubt. Spiritual law says that it is never too late to mend, and that when we seek God's help we find it.

Look unto me, and be ye saved, all the ends of the earth; for I am God, and there is none else (Isaiah 45:22).

No matter what problem you may have to face today, there is a solution, because you have nothing to deal with but your own thoughts. As you know, you have the power to select and control your thoughts, difficult though it may be at times to do so. As long as you think that your destiny is in the hands of other people, the situation is hopeless.

Remind yourself constantly that you have nothing to deal with but your own thoughts. Write it down where you will see it often. Have it on your desk. Hang it in your bedroom. Write it in your pocketbook. Write it on your soul. It will transform your life. It will lead you out of the land of Egypt and out of the House of Bondage. It will bring you to God.

I thought on my ways, and turned my feet unto thy testimonies (Psalm 119:59).

Read Acts 19:1–41.

This is an extremely colorful and dramatic chapter even for the Bible, which is so full of color and drama. Every problem has a solution. Some problems last a long time, some a short time, but always there is a solution, and *always the solution is to turn from the outer to the inner.* When you admire some outer, passing thing too much, and thus give power to the manifestation, you are saying, "Great is Diana." When you fear some outer thing or condition or person, then you are also saying, "Great is Diana." And when you say, "Great is Diana," then your troubles really begin.

The First Commandment is, "I am the Lord thy God"—God, spirit, nothing outside. There is not a single mistake that you or I have ever made, there is not a single trouble or heartache that has ever come to us, that has not come directly through saying, "Great is Diana," and forgetting God.

Great is our Lord, and of great power: his understanding is infinite (Psalm 147:5).

The spiritual forces that created and sustain the whole universe are available to help you at any time—provided you call upon them intelligently. The way to call upon this Power is to become quiet both mentally and physically, and then to call upon *it* quietly to do what *it* knows to be necessary. Do not dictate ways and means.

Have you ever seen a huge hoist in action at the docks? You know what happens. The operator would not dream of trying to pull up that load with his muscles. He would damage himself seriously and make no impression on the task in hand. What he does is to gently throw a small switch—and leave it in. Then the electric power raises the load to any height required.

When you work spiritually you are applying Infinite Power to your problem, and there can be but one outcome—victory.

Great in counsel and mighty in work: for thine eyes are open upon all the ways of the sons of men (Jeremiah 32:19).

If you have explored some of the back waters within a few miles of the ocean you will know how much difference tidal water makes. Here you come upon a stagnant pool, partly covered with weeds and slime, an unpleasant place to be near. Not far away is another pool but this is filled with clean, salt-smelling sea water, and the growing things around it are pleasant and wholesome. The difference is that in one case the living ocean water pours in twice a day charged with vitality, and then flows out again carrying away anything stale or lifeless. It is this circulation of life that makes the difference between the two pools.

When the tide is out, we sometimes see a boat stranded, unable to move, but we know that this condition is only temporary because the tide always comes back and refloats the boat. As long as you keep up your daily visit with God, your soul is open to tidal water, and even if you should seemingly be left high and dry for a period, it is only a question of time before the living ocean will float you off once more.

Keep your soul flooded with the *tidal water* of eternal life and

. . . *nothing shall by any means hurt you* (Luke 10:19).

People sometimes say, "I believe firmly in the spiritual teaching, and I have done so for years, but I have never been able to make it work—isn't that strange?" And sometimes they say this with quite an air of triumph.

Such people remind me of a man who used to boast that he had an ailment that no one could heal. He had successfully defied every school of healing and had emerged triumphantly still in possession of his affliction. As it happens, his wife did heal him later on by prayer alone, but she was a patient and persevering woman. That man's wife probably points the way to the overcoming of such illogicality. The key to success lies in just the qualities that she obviously had; patience combined with a gentle and unhurried expectation of success.

The patient whom she healed is not a rare specimen, nor is he unknown to any one of us. We are all likely to encounter him under our own hat at any moment!

I know thy works, and charity, and service, and faith, and thy patience, and thy works . . . (Revelation 2:19).

Volumes have been written on the secret of happiness, but I like the simple old story that has been told so often.

In the old days, there was a king who was so miserable and unhappy that he called together all of his soothsayers, magicians, and other court advisers to find a remedy. They tried all sorts of methods to rouse the king out of his deep despair—but alas, to no avail. Finally, one of them suggested that a search be made for the happiest man in the kingdom, for it was thought that if the king could put on the man's undershirt, he would become happy too. In due course, the happiest man in the kingdom was found. But, of course, he had never even owned an undershirt. His happiness sprang from within.

And ye shall seek me, and find me, when ye shall search for me with all your heart (Jeremiah 29:13).

Within you is an inexhaustible source of power, if you can but contact it. That power can heal you, and it can inspire you by telling you what to do and how to do it. It can give you peace of mind, and, above all, it can give you direct knowledge of God. That power is scientific prayer. There is no problem that prayer cannot overcome and no good thing that it cannot bring into your life.

This is the message of the whole Bible. It was summed up by Jesus when he said,

. . . the kingdom of God is within you (Luke 17:21).

This truth was dramatically illustrated by an incident in real life. The body of a tramp, clad in rags, was discovered near a lime kiln where he had evidently crept for warmth. After the autopsy his clothes were torn up to be put into the incinerator, and sewn into the lining of the trousers was a bank note for a large amount. Unquestionably the original owner of the suit had had it sewn in there for safety, and for some unknown reason lost track of it.

Consider the situation! This poor hobo had sat down many a time to lukewarm coffee—and all the time he was sitting on a thousand dollars. People may have plenty of money and yet be hoboes for health or happiness or spiritual experience. Riches do not become wealth until they are realized. Cash your bill at the Bank of Heaven and make it productive.

But my God shall supply all your need . . . (Philippians 4:19).

Many people say to me, "I want to get on faster. I want more understanding." And as a rule they go on to ask for a list of books to read or some "advanced course" that they can take.

This attitude is quite mistaken. It implies that spiritual advancement is a question of intellectual activity—of the mere accretion of knowledge. That is true in the study of mathematics, or of physics, or chemistry, but it is not true in metaphysics. Spiritual growth comes from putting into practice the knowledge we already possess. Instead of reading another book, read your favorite book once more and apply it more carefully than ever in your practical life.

Metaphysics, like music, is both a science and an art. In metaphysics it is absolutely true that you learn by doing.

. . . *be ye doers of the word, and not hearers only* . . . (James 1:22).

A good housekeeper sees to it that dust and dirt do not accumulate in nooks and corners and on shelves. Periodically, the house is gone over and given a thorough cleaning. Too often in our spiritual lives, we allow negative things to accumulate in the corners of our minds. We tackle the obvious problems as they come along, but allow the small difficulties to pile up in the corners.

For instance, if we are faced with a problem of health or finance, we get to work on that immediately, but if, on the other hand, someone has injured us, instead of handling the incident spiritually at the time, we tuck it away and perhaps pack in a little resentment along with it. Such problems should be dealt with as they arise. If someone has injured you, forgive him now, and be done with it. Take care of the other difficulties in like manner.

Be a good housekeeper. Clean out every nook and corner—and God will make you worthy of greater accomplishments in the future.

And he said unto him, Well done, thou good servant: because thou hast been faithful in a very little, have thou authority over ten cities (Luke 19:17).

When you apply a certain word to God, it must bear the same essential meaning as it does when you apply it to man—otherwise it has no meaning at all. When you say that God is *Love* or *Intelligence*, or that He is *just*, these words must mean substantially what they mean when applied to human beings. The love of God must be essentially the same thing that we know as the love of the mother for her children, or the love of the artist for his creation, purified and increased to infinity, of course.

Many people say that God is Love, and at the same time maintain that He visits finite sin with eternal punishment. They claim that God is just, and yet maintain that people living today are suffering disabilities for a sin supposed to have been committed by Adam thousands of years before they were born.

The truth is that God *is* Love and Intelligence; and that He works with perfect wisdom and perfect justice to all, at all times, in the ordinary and correct meaning of these words.

. . . *God is light, and in Him is no darkness at all* (1 John 1:5).

He that loveth not knoweth not God; for God is Love (1 John 4:8).

Good and upright is the Lord . . . (Psalm 25:8).

When you give your mental assent to any idea, good or bad, you associate yourself with that idea and you incorporate it into your consciousness—to the extent that you realize it. When you read a passage of Scripture you will, if you assent to it mentally, incorporate it into your life to that extent.

This law, of course, works the other way too. If when you hear or read of some piece of injustice or cruelty, you approve it mentally by thinking that "it serves him right," you are associating yourself with that deed, and making it a part of your own life, even though you do not speak a word. It is the mental assent that counts.

Give your assent only to Truth.

For I delight in the law of God after the inward man: But I see another law in my numbers, warring against the law of my mind, and bringing me into captivity. . . . So then with the mind I myself serve the law of God . . . (Romans 7:22, 23, 25).

Resignation in defeat is really a sin.

If an old problem continues to stick—pray for inspiration and intelligence. Stop struggling and thank God constantly for setting you free.

If nervous or frightened—throw the responsibility on God, and tell Him that you know you are safe in His hands.

If someone is being troublesome—see only the Presence of God where the troublesome person seems to be.

If you want to make faster progress—claim understanding and affirm that divine Love is working through you.

Casting all your care upon him; for he careth for you (1 Peter 5:7).

We do not have to create good. We do not have to persuade God to be Love, or Life, or Truth, or Intelligence. We do not have to ask Him to remember us. We could not ask for any good. Fundamentally, evil is a false belief about the power and availability of good.

If we draw down the shades in every room in a house, that house will be in darkness, and is likely to become damp and unhealthy as well, no matter how brightly the sun may be shining outside. Salvation consists in raising these shades and opening the windows—then He does the rest.

    . . . *walk as children of light* (Ephesians 5:8).

When you are praying for your true place, it is well to remember that the full demonstration may not come in one move, but more likely after a series of stages.

Now, if you despise these intermediate steps, and think "this is a little better, but it is not really what I want," you will keep the demonstration back. Neither should you accept a small improvement as being all that you can hope to get. The scientific attitude is to see the stepping stone *as* stepping stone; to bless it, and give thanks for it, and to continue praying for the next step.

For precept must be upon precept . . . line upon line, here a little, and there a little (Isaiah 28:10).

Regeneration means building a new mentality; that is, creating a new soul in place of your present one. It does not mean merely improving your present self—it means producing (through the power of God, of course), a new self.

If you do this, everything else in your life will rapidly change for the better. Other people will become much more friendly to you. Because your soul will be filled with peace, you will radiate peace, and other people will get it intuitively. Everybody likes peace and harmony and they are attracted to any source from which it comes.

Naturally you cannot radiate peace if you do not first possess it within yourself. You cannot radiate anything from the outside. To radiate any quality, that quality must be within yourself.

True peace of mind is the short cut to regeneration. The Master said,

Peace I leave with you, my peace I give unto you (John 14:27).

> Into the hand that made the rose,
> shall I with trembling fall?
> —George Meredith

There is absolutely no reason to fear death. The same God is on the other side of the grave as on this side. However, most people do fear death, partly as fear of the unknown, and partly as the result of false teaching. Actually there is no death in the sense of extinction.

To understand death, you have to realize that you really possess not one body but two. You have not only the physical body, but also a second body made of a form of energy too fine to be seen. This etheric body interpenetrates the physical body as air fills a sponge. There are people who can see the etheric body because they have the power of contacting much finer vibrations than can be perceived by the ordinary physical senses.

It is this etheric body that is the repository of all your thoughts and feelings. It is the "psyche" of the psychologist. That is why personality survives death; because it resides in the etheric that passes over intact, and not in the physical that breaks up into decomposition.

During sleep, trance, and under anesthesia, when the etheric may leave the physical body, it remains attached to it by an etheric ligament called in the Bible the Silver Cord. The cord is so elastic that the etheric body can go very long distances and still remain attached to the physical corpus.

Death is the severing of the Silver Cord. When the Silver Cord is severed, an individual falls into a state of unconsciousness that may last for minutes, days, or even weeks. Then he wakens as from sleep, and his new life has begun.

The next world is actually all around us here. The so-called dead are carrying on their lives here where we are now, but in their own world and in their own way. The reason we do not see them around us or collide with them is the same reason that one radio program does not interfere with another—they are on different wavelengths.

. . . though I walk through the valley of the shadow of death, I will fear no evil: for thou art with me . . . (Psalm 23).

Perhaps the most startling change that the discarnate has to meet is the fact that thought is the normal means of communication, and therefore there is no deception. You pass for what you are and that is the end of matter.

What is it that determines the kind of place to which you will go after death and the sort of people among whom you will find yourself? You will go to the sort of place and be among the sort of people for whom you have prepared yourself by your habitual thinking and your mode of living while on this earth. Remember that death makes positively no change in you; you are just the same person that you were before it happened. No one "sends" you anywhere. You naturally gravitate to the place where you belong.

You do not "meet God" on the next plane any more than you do on this plane. Of course, He is fully present on the next plane just as He is on this plane; but there as here, He is to be contacted only in one's own consciousness. Heaven is that perfect state of consciousness in which one is in full realization of the divine Presence. If you can reach to that level of consciousness while still in this world (and a few have succeeded in doing so), you are in heaven now and your awareness of God will be intensified after death.

However, there are some very unpleasant localities in the next world and people whose minds are chiefly given up to hatred, deceit, or sensuality, will find themselves in such places. These are the places referred to as "hell."

Consider the man or woman who lives wholly for the body and is dominated by it. Physical cravings, being part of the mentality, are, of course, carried over to the next plane, but there there is no physical body through which these appetites may be satisfied, and so the victim is tormented by desire but unable to satisfy it, until, in the course of time, these desires fade out by starvation. This is the natural punishment for allowing the physical body to assume control, and surely it is punishment enough.

For we know that if our earthly house of this tabernacle were dissolved, we have a building of God, a house not made with hands, eternal in the heavens (2 Corinthians 5:1).

Will you meet your relatives and friends when you go over? Where there is a strong emotional link either of love or hatred there is likely to be a meeting. Where there is a strong link of genuine love there is sure to be a meeting. Where there is no particular feeling between two people there will not be a meeting. There is a real danger that if you allow yourself to indulge in hatred of anyone, you will meet when you have both passed over. To prevent this happening, destroy the link by ceasing to hate.

The so-called dead are very sensitive to our thoughts, and for this reason excessive grief is to be deprecated. It saddens them and prevents their focusing their attention as they should upon the new life that they are starting. Of course, it seems very hard to tell people not to grieve when one whom they have dearly loved passes out of sight, but remember that if there is a link of love you will certainly meet again, and that nothing that is good, or beautiful, or true, can ever be lost.

We can pray for those who have passed on, and indeed it is a sacred duty to do so. The practice was generally discontinued after the Reformation because it had been greatly abused and commercialized, but, nevertheless, it is an excellent practice in itself. Realize peace of mind, freedom, and understanding for them.

In my Father's house are many mansions: if it were not so, I would have told you. I go to prepare a place for you (John 14:2).

Some thought should be given to the fate of those who commit suicide. The majority of those who take their own lives are so terrorized at the time that they are not entirely responsible for the act. Such people fare on the other side like anyone else. Conscious and intentional self-destruction is a refusal to meet the problems of life, and obviously it cannot be possible to do that successfully. These persons are apt to find themselves in a confused mental state. Of course, they can be greatly helped by prayer, as can all others. Ultimately they have to face all over again precisely the kind of problem they have run away from.

Like as a father pitieth his children, so the Lord pitieth them that fear Him. For He knoweth our frame; he remembereth that we are dust (Psalm 103:13–14).

. . . the goodness of God endureth . . . (Psalm 51:1).

Is it possible to communicate with those who have passed on into the next world? Extremists on one side say dogmatically that it is absolutely impossible to do so. Enthusiasts on the other side claim that their deceased friends direct their actions. The truth is that communication does take place, but that the wise dead understand the necessity of our exercising our own power of choice and do not intrude. But they do often come to our aid.

If you wish to investigate psychic things, do so thoroughly and scientifically. The chief objection to the running after mediums is that it may become a running away from the responsibilities of this life. Thus seeking mediums becomes what is called in psychology an escape mechanism. Your business is to face up to your problems and to try to solve them.

There is a truly spiritual mode of communication from which nothing but good can come. It is this: Sit down quietly and remind yourself that the one God really is Omnipresent. Then reflect that your real self is in the Presence of God now, and that the real self of your loved one is also in the Presence of God. Do this for a few minutes every day, and sooner or later you will get a sense of communication.

For to this end Christ both died, and rose . . . that he might be Lord both of the dead and living (Romans 14:9).

Pass a test in Spiritual understanding, and never again throughout eternity will that particular task have to be done. Your attitude should be:

I am going to live forever; in a thousand years from now I shall still be alive and active somewhere; in a hundred thousand years still alive and active somewhere; and so the events of today have only the importance that belongs to today. I greet the unknown with a cheer, and press forward joyously, exulting in the great adventure.

Armed with this philosophy, and really understanding its power, you have nothing to fear in life or death—because God is All, and God is Good.

Now the God of peace, that brought again from the dead our Lord Jesus . . . make you perfect in every good work to do his will, working in you that which is well-pleasing in his sight . . . (Hebrews 13:20–21).

RESURGAM

There is no death! The stars go down
To rise upon some other shore,
And bright in heaven's jeweled crown
They shine for evermore.

Time is no death! The dust we tread
Shall change beneath the summer showers
To golden grain, or mellow fruit,
Or rainbow-tinted flowers.
And ever near us, though unseen,
The dear immortal spirits tread;
For all the boundless universe
Is life—there are no dead!
                    —John Luckey McCreery,
                        "There Is No Death"

O death, where is thy sting? O grave, where is thy victory? . . . But thanks be to God, which giveth us the victory through our Lord Jesus Christ (1 Corinthians 15:55, 57).

What is nature? What we call nature is a small part of God's universe that we are able to see at the present time, and much of which we see awry. All the wonderful things that are going on in the woods, all the marvelous happenings that take place in the depths of the ocean, the whole sublime story of the heavens, are all parts of God's self-expression. Above all, our own bodies themselves are part of nature, perhaps the most wonderful part of all; and probably the part about which we ourselves know least.

But ask now the beasts, and they shall teach thee; and the fowls of the air, and they shall tell thee: Or speak to the earth, and it shall teach thee: and the fishes of the sea shall declare unto thee. Who knoweth not in all these that the hand of the Lord hath wrought this? In whose hand is the soul of every living thing and the breath of all mankind. . . . With him is wisdom and strength, he hath counsel and understanding (Job 12:7–10, 13).

Have you ever asked yourself why there should be such a difference between one human lot and another? Have you ever wondered why some people seem to be so happy and fortunate in their lives, while others appear to undergo so much undeserved suffering? To the honest and fearless soul, the problem of the inequality of human lives is one that clamors for solution.

Men and women are not born free and equal. They are created free and equal, but they are not born free and equal. They start this life like horses in a handicap race—no two bearing an equal burden. Now, why should this be, if indeed God is Love, and if God is just, and if God is all-powerful?

The answer is that this life that you are living today is not the only life, and that it cannot be understood or judged by itself. You have lived before, in different ages and in different civilizations. Some of those who are at the bottom of the social ladder today have walked the earth as kings, and generals, and high priests; and some who now sit in the seats of the mighty have toiled as peasants, or worn the chains of the slave. And you, yourself, in future ages, will very likely return to this earth planet and live out another life. The conditions under which you start that life will be the outcome of the lives you have already lived; but most particularly will they be the outcome of the life that you are living at the present. What is customarily called a lifetime is really but a comparatively brief day in a long, long life, and the circumstances into which you were born are the natural outcome of the way in which you have lived and comported yourself in your former lives. You are reaping today the results of the seeds that you have sown during these many previous lives.

. . . *He which soweth sparingly shall reap also sparingly, and he which soweth bountifully shall reap also bountifully* (2 Corinthians 9:6).

When you understand that this present life is only one day in your *long* life, and that at the change called death you simply disappear unto the next plane, to come back again later on—perhaps several hundred years later—then the events of this particular life appear in their true proportion, and then you begin to have dominion. The events of this life will not appear less important because of your new knowledge, but they will no longer intimidate you, because you will know that you can control them. No seeming misfortune will any longer have power to break your heart or weaken your courage. You will understand life as the wondrous opportunity and the glorious gift that it is.

It is true that when you return you will have to meet the same types of problems but the conditions will be utterly different. Also, you will probably meet some of your present associates again, particularly if there is an emotional link either of love or hatred between you. Love will take care of itself; but you must get all hatred out of your heart, if you do not want to renew disagreeable contacts.

A thorough understanding of this doctrine makes us more tolerant. It leads us to do everything we can to make the path of others easier so as to facilitate their personal evolution and that of the race. In our own lives we face up to our difficulties courageously, knowing that to run away is to postpone the day of reckoning.

. . . *all the churches shall know that I am he which searcheth the reins and hearts: and I will give unto every one of you according to your works* (Revelation 2:23).

Why is reincarnation necessary? Why do we come back for short excursions of perhaps seventy or eighty years instead of, let us say, living one very long lifetime of perhaps a thousand or even several thousand years?

The explanation lies in man's reluctance to adopt new ideas and adapt himself to changing conditions. In each new experience, however, he wants to do things in new ways; then as the years of his maturity go by, the strong race suggestions all around him gradually get their way. He begins to acquire vested interests (mentally) in the status quo. The only remedy, when crystallization sets in, is to remove him from the earth plane altogether; send him to the etheric planes for rest, reflection, assimilation, and general readjustment; and then bring him back once more as a baby, to experience a new youth and a new period of true spiritual production.

There are other reasons why multiple lives are necessary. You need to develop every side of your character. You need to learn lessons of discipline and self-restraint, and you need to learn to use authority in the right way. You need to learn the lesson of getting on with other people, and you must also learn to be alone. You must learn to bear failure and disappointment with fortitude and you must learn to stand success without allowing your head to be turned. You have to learn both patience and the lesson of enterprise and adventure. Above all, you have to move about in time and space so that you may learn that nothing God made is really foreign or separate—and this could not be done in one lifetime.

Wherefore the law was our schoolmaster to bring us unto Christ . . . (Galatians 3:24).

181

J ust as like attracts like, so like produces like. This is a cosmic law, which means that it is universally true throughout the whole of existence right up through the higher planes. As Jesus put it, you do not gather grapes from thorns or figs from thistles; and he also said,

Even so every good tree bringeth forth good fruit; but a corrupt tree bringeth forth evil fruit . . . (Matthew 7:17).

So it is with our thoughts and words and deeds. As we sow so shall we reap, sometimes almost immediately, sometimes after a long interval. But always, sooner or later *like produces like*.

Reincarnation also explains the differences in talents that we find between one man and another. The born musician is a man who has studied music in a previous life, perhaps in several lives, and has therefore built that faculty into his soul. He is a talented musician today because he is reaping what he sowed yesterday. In the East this law of sowing and reaping is known as karma and the term is a convenient one.

Note carefully, however, that karma is not punishment. If you touch a red hot stove, you will burn your finger. This will hurt you, but it is not punishment, only a benign and reformative consequence, for after one or two such experiences in childhood, you learn to keep your fingers away from hot iron. So it is with all natural retribution— you suffer because you have a lesson to learn.

Why do you not remember your previous lives? Consider how prone people are to worry and grieve foolishly over the past events of this one life, and imagine their state if they had the material of many lives to handle in this way.

And so the past is mercifully withheld from us until we reach the stage when we can regard our own histories impersonally and objectively, and when we do reach that stage it is possible to remember our previous lives.

> Our birth is but a sleep and a forgetting,
>   The soul that rises with us, our life's Star,
>   Hath had elsewhere its setting,
>   And cometh from afar;
>   Not in entire forgetfulness,
>   And not in utter darkness,
> But trailing clouds of glory, do we come
>   From God, who is our home.
>   —Wordsworth

Is it absolutely necessary to come back? The answer is that you need not come back if you will concentrate your whole heart upon God, and seek His Presence until you realize it completely. If you can do this, of all tasks the most difficult, then you will leave this earth planet to enter into full communion with God, and you need never come back. Hardly anyone, however, is able to do this at present, and so we have to go on by stages, learning from experience, study, prayer, and meditation; living life after life until at last we "grow up" spiritually.

. . . *I trust in the mercy of the Lord forever and ever* (Psalm 52:8).

An old adage says: "God has a plan for every man, and He has one for you." Your real problem—the only problem you have—is to find your true calling in life. Everything else will fall into place. You will be happy; and upon happiness, health will follow. You will have all the supply that you require to meet your needs, and this means that you will have perfect freedom; for poverty and freedom cannot go together.

God has not made you without a definite purpose in view. The Universe is a universe; that is, it is a unified harmony, a divine scheme. It could not happen, therefore, that God could create a spiritual entity such as you are, without having a special purpose in view, a special place for you. Whatever the place may be, there can be only one person who can fill it perfectly.

But how is one to find his true place in life? Is there any means whereby you may discover what it really is that God wishes you to do? The answer is divinely simple—already from time to time, God Himself has whispered into your heart just that very wonderful thing, nothing less than what is called your heart's desire. The most secret wish that lies at the bottom of your heart, that is just the very thing that God is wishing you to do or to be for Him. And the birth of that wish in your soul was the voice of God Himself telling you to arise and come up higher because He had need of you.

Delight thyself also in the Lord, and he shall give thee the desires of thine heart (Psalm 37:4).

If you say that you are unhappy, dissatisfied, perhaps ill or impoverished, a failure, this is simply another way of putting the fact that you are not allowing the will of God to have free play in your life—you are not doing the thing that He meant you to do.

Discontent is not necessarily a bad thing. It is your duty to be discontented with anything less than complete harmony and happiness. A wholesome discontent with dullness, failure, and frustration is your incentive for overcoming such things. Whoever you are, your true place is calling, and, because you really are a spark of the Divine, you will never be content until you answer.

Remember that this call is the call of God, and when God calls you to His Service, He pays all the expenses. Whatever you may require to answer that call—all will He furnish, if you be about His business and not your own.

Ye have not chosen me, but I have chosen you, and ordained you, that ye should go and bring forth fruit, and that your fruit should remain (John 15:16).

As far as God is concerned, there is no check of any kind upon the amount of divine energy that we can appropriate, or, therefore, upon the things that we can do or be. Yet, for practical purposes, you can draw from the inexhaustible Source only in accordance with the measure of your understanding, just as you can draw water from the Atlantic only in accordance with the size of the vessel that you use. Almost everyone is foolishly content to fill his pitcher, small as it may be, to somewhere very short of the top.

The true manner of God's working is illustrated by a simple anecdote. A certain man was working in his garden, assisted by his little girl who had undertaken the task of watering the lawn by means of the usual rubber hose. Suddenly she cried out: "Daddy, the water has stopped." The father looked over, and, taking in the situation quietly, said, "Well, take your foot off the hose."

The ultimate cause of all our troubles is just this. Behind all secondary and proximate causes lies the same primary mistake. We have been pressing our feet and the whole weight of our mentality upon the pipe line of life, and then complaining because the water does not flow.

And the Lord shall guide thee continually, and satisfy thy soul in drought . . . and thou shalt be like a watered garden, and like a spring of water, whose waters fail not (Isaiah 58:11).

Jesus has told us that we always demonstrate our consciousness. We always demonstrate what we habitually have in our mind. What sort of mind have you? Do not let anyone else tell you, because they do not know. People who like you will think your mentality is better than it is; those who do not like you will think it is worse. Just examine your conditions and see what you are demonstrating. This method is scientific and infallible.

If an automobile engineer is working out a new design for an engine, for instance, he doesn't say: "I wonder what Smith thinks about this. I like Smith. If Smith is against this I won't try it." Nor does he say, "I won't try this idea because it comes from France." He is impersonal and unemotional about it. He says, "I will test it out, and decide by the results I obtain." All that anyone can do for you is to help you change your thought. You yourself must keep it changed. No one else can think for you. "No man can save his brother's soul or pay his brother's debt."

. . . and I will put a new spirit within you . . . (Ezekiel 11:19).

Here is one way of solving a problem by scientific prayer.

Get by yourself, and be quiet for a few moments. Do not strain to think rightly or to find the right thought, but just be quiet. Remind yourself that the Bible says "Be still, and know that I am God."

Then begin to think about God. Remind yourself of some of the things that you know about Him—that he is present everywhere, that He knows you and loves you and cares for you. Read a few verses of the Bible, or a paragraph from any spiritual book that helps you.

During this state it is important not to think about your problem, but *to give your attention to God*. In other words, do not try to solve your problem directly (which would be using will power) but rather become interested in thinking of the nature of God.

Next claim the thing that you need. Claim it quietly and confidently, as you would ask for something to which you are entitled. Then give thanks for the accomplished fact as you would if somebody handed you a gift. Jesus said when you pray, believe that you receive and you shall receive.

Do not discuss your treatment with anyone.

In quietness and in confidence shall be your strength . . . (Isaiah 30:15).

Why not make the following experiment, which will not only be thrillingly interesting, but will certainly teach you more in one day than you could learn from books or lectures in many weeks.

Here is what you have to do. For one whole day think, speak, and act exactly as you would if you were absolutely convinced of the truth of the statements that God has all *power* and infinite *intelligence*, and that His nature is infinite *goodness* and love.

To think in this manner all day will be the most difficult thing, because thought is so subtle. To speak in accordance with these truths will be easier, if you are vigilant. To act in accordance with them will be the easiest part, although it may require much in the way of moral courage.

And being fully persuaded that, what he had promised, he was able also to perform (Romans 4:21).

People who are honestly trying to follow the spiritual life often make the mistake of being too hard on themselves. Because they do not seem to be progressing as fast as they would naturally like, or because they find themselves repeating some old fault that they thought they had completely overcome, they feel discouraged, and condemn themselves mercilessly.

All this is foolish. If you are doing your best to use what Truth you know, at present, you are doing all that you have a right to expect of yourself.

Don't be impatient with yourself—but this does not mean that you are to be lazy or complacent. Handle yourself as a wise parent handles an obstreperous child—kindly, patiently, but with gentle firmness, not expecting too much too quickly, but foreseeing inevitable growth and improvement.

. . . and all of you are children of the most high (Psalm 82:6).

Read Matthew 7:1–5.

These few verses consist of only about one hundred words, and yet it is hardly too much to say that at their simple face value they comprise the most staggering document ever presented to mankind. In these five verses we are told more about the nature of man and the meaning of life, and the importance of conduct, and the art of living, and the secret of happiness and success, and the way out of trouble, and the approach to God, and the emancipation of the soul, and the salvation of the world, than all the philosophers and the theologians and the savants put together have told us—for it explains the Great Law. "Burn the rest of the books, for it is all in this one," would hold in reference to those words.

People are very apt to think, especially when they are strongly tempted, that they can probably escape the clutches of authority in some other way. If, however, they understood that the law of retribution is a cosmic law, impersonal and unchanging as the law of gravity, they would think twice before they treated other people unjustly. The law of gravity is never off duty, and no one would ever dream of trying to evade it, or coax it, or bribe it, or intimidate it. People accept it as being inevitable and shape their conduct accordingly—and the law of retribution is even as the law of gravity.

You may like or dislike the law, and if you wish, you may try to ignore it; but you cannot deny that Jesus Christ taught it, and in the most direct and emphatic way when he said:

Judge not, that ye be not judged. For with what judgment ye judge, ye shall be judged (Matthew 7:1–2).

With what measure ye mete, it shall be measured to you again (Matthew 7:2).

If the average man understood for a moment the meaning of these words, they would turn his everyday conduct inside out, and so change him that, in a comparatively short space of time, his closest friends would hardly know him.

The plain fact is that it is the law of life that, as we think, and speak, and act toward others, so will others think, and speak, and act toward us. Everything that we do to others will sooner or later be done to us by someone, somewhere. Perhaps by someone who knows nothing of our previous action, but for every unkind word that we speak to or about another person, an unkind word will be spoken to or about us. For every time that we cheat, we will be cheated. Every time we neglect a duty, or evade a responsibility, or misuse authority over other people, we are doing something for which we will inevitably have to pay by suffering a like injury ourself.

However, it is a poor law that does not work both ways, and so it is equally true that for every good deed that you do, for every kind word that you speak, you will in the same way, at some time or other, get back an equivalent.

The Golden Rule in Scientific Christianity is: *Think about others as you would wish them to think about you.* In the light of the knowledge that we now possess, the observance of this rule becomes a very solemn duty, but, more than that indeed, it is a debt of honor.

The student having now gained an understanding of what the Great Law is and how it works, is in a position to take the next great step and understand how it is possible to rise above even the Great Law itself, in the name of the CHRIST.

This does not mean that the laws of the physical or mental planes are broken. It means that man, because of his essential divine self-hood, has the power of rising above these domains into the infinite dimension of Spirit where such laws no longer affect him. The law of reaping what one sows, often called the Law of Karma, is actually law for mind only; it is not law for Spirit. In Spirit all is perfect and eternal, unchanging good.

So man has the choice of Karma or Christ. This is the best news that has ever come to mankind, and for that reason it is called the glad tidings, or the Gospel. Karma turns out to be inexorable only so long as you do not pray. For any given mistake, you must either suffer the consequences, which we call being punished, or wipe them out by the Practice of the Presence of God.

It must not be supposed, however, that the consequences of a mistake are to be cheaply evaded by a perfunctory prayer. Sufficient realization of God to alter fundamentally the character of the sinner is required in order to wipe out the punishment that otherwise must always follow upon sin. When the sinner becomes a changed man, and will not even desire to repeat his sin, then is he saved, for Christ is Lord of Karma.

And be not conformed to this world: but be ye transformed by the renewing of your mind, that ye may prove what is that good, and acceptable, and perfect, will of God (Romans 12:2).

Give not that which is holy unto the dogs, neither cast ye your pearls before swine, lest they trample them under their feet, and turn again and rend you (Matthew 7:6).

Intelligence is just as essential a part of the Christian message as is love. God is love, but God is also infinite intelligence, and unless these two qualities are balanced in our lives, we do not get wisdom; for wisdom is the perfect blending of intelligence and love. Love without intelligence may do much undesigned harm—and intelligence without love may ultimate in clever cruelty. All true Christian activity will express wisdom.

Never rely upon your own judgment to say who is ready for the Truth and who is not, but rely for guidance upon the inspiration of the Holy Spirit. If you are praying regularly every day for wisdom, and fresh opportunities for service, the right people will be brought to you.

Remember that those with whom you associate closely will have your personal conduct under constant inspection. The quickest way to spread the Truth is by living the life yourself. Then people will notice the change in you and they will come round of their own accord, begging to share your secret.

Read Matthew 7:7–11.

This is the wonderful passage in which Jesus enunciates the primary truth of the Fatherhood of God. He says here, definitely and clearly, that the real relationship of God and man is that of parent and child. It is extremely difficult to realize the far-reaching importance that this declaration holds for the life of the soul.

It is axiomatic, of course, that the offspring must be of the same nature and species as the parent; and so if God and man are indeed Father and child, man must be essentially divine too, and susceptible of infinite development up the rising pathway of divinity. That is to say, as man's true nature unfolds, he will expand in spiritual consciousness until he has transcended all bounds of human imagination. It is in reference to our glorious destiny, that Jesus himself says elsewhere, quoting the older scriptures:

Jesus answered them, Is it not written in your law, I said, Ye are gods?

If he called them gods, unto whom the word of God came, and the scripture cannot be broken . . . (John 10:34–35).

If ye then, being evil, know how to give good gifts unto your children, how much more shall your Father which is in heaven give good things to them that ask Him? (Matthew 7:11).

We are the children of God; and if children, then sons, and joint heirs with Jesus Christ, as Paul says. At the present time we find ourselves full of limitations and disabilities because we are spiritually but children—minors. Children are irresponsible, lacking in wisdom and experience, and have to be kept under control lest their mistakes should entail serious consequences to themselves.

. . . That the heir, as long as he is a child, differeth nothing from a servant, though he be lord of all;

But is under tutors and governors . . . (Galatians 4:1).

But when the fullness of time is come, he realizes that it is the voice of God Himself that is in his heart, making him cry: "Abba Father." Then at last he knows that he is the son of a great king, and that all his Father has is his for the using, whether it be health, or supply, or opportunity, or beauty, or joy, or any other of the thoughts of God.

The most mischievous thing in life is man's reluctance to perceive his own dominion. God has given us dominion over all things, but we shrink like frightened children from assuming it, although that assuming is the one and only escape for us.

Jesus, who knew the human heart, and understood our weakness in this respect, commands us,

Ask, and it shall be given you; seek, and ye shall find; knock, and it shall be opened unto you:

For every one that asketh receiveth; and he that seeketh findeth; and to him that knocketh it shall be opened (Matthew 7:7–8).

Is not this the Magna Carta of personal freedom for every man, woman, and child on earth? Is not this the decree of the emancipation of the slaves of every kind of bondage, physical, mental, or spiritual? We have no business to accept ill-health, or poverty, or sinfulness, or strife, or unhappiness, or remorse, with resignation. We have no right to accept anything less than freedom and harmony and joy, for only with these things do we glorify God, and express His holy will, which is our *raison d'être*.

We are to reorganize our lives in accordance with his teaching, continuously and untiringly until our goal is attained. That this attainment, that our victory over every negative condition is not merely possible but is definitely promised to us, finds its proof in these glorious words.

Therefore all things whatsoever ye would that men should do to you, do ye even so to them: for this is the law of the prophets (Matthew 7:12).

Here in the sublime precept that we call the Golden Rule, Jesus reiterates that great Law in a concise summing up. This repetition follows upon his wonderful statement of the fatherhood of God. The underlying explanation for the existence of the great law is the fact that we are fundamentally all parts of the Great Mind. Because we are all ultimately one, to hurt another is really to hurt oneself, and to help another is really to help oneself. The fatherhood of God compels us to accept the brotherhood of man, and spiritually, brotherhood is unity.

*E*nter ye in at the strait gate: for wide is the gate, and broad is the way, that leadeth to destruction, and many there be which go in thereat:

Because strait is the gate, and narrow is the way, which leadeth unto life, and few there be that find it (Matthew 7:13–14).

There is only one way under the sun by which man can attain salvation, in the true sense of the word, and that is by bringing about a radical and permanent change for the better in his own consciousness. For countless generations humanity has been trying in every other conceivable way to compass its own good. This change in consciousness is the *strait gate* that Jesus speaks of here, and, as he says, the number of those who find it is comparatively small.

Now why should man be so reluctant, apparently, to try to change his consciousness? The answer is that the changing of one's consciousness is really very hard work, calling for constant unceasing vigilance and a breaking of mental habits. Entering the strait gait is, however, worth much more than whatever trouble or effort it may call for.

If you make a *qualitative* change in consciousness, which is what happens in prayer, then not only is the effect of that change felt in every department of your life, but it is with you through all eternity, for you never can lose it. *Thieves cannot break in and steal.*

As soon as you obtain this spiritual consciousness you will find that all things indeed work together for good to those who love God.

A tragic mistake that is often made is to assume that the will of God is bound to be something very dull and uninviting, if not positively unpleasant. Consciously or not some persons look upon God as a hard taskmaster, or a severe parent. Too often their prayers amount to something like this: "Please God, give me such-and-such a boon, which I sorely need—but I don't suppose you will, because you won't think it is good for me." Needless to say, a prayer of this sort is answered as all prayers are answered, according to the faith of the subject; that is to say, the boon is not granted. The truth is that the will of God for us always means greater freedom, greater self-expression, newer and brighter experience, wider opportunity of service to others—life more abundant.

God is love; and he that dwelleth in love dwelleth in God, and God in him (1 John 4:16).

Read Matthew 7:15–20.

If man really were left without a simple practical test of religious truth, he would assuredly be in a sad plight; but happily this is not the case. Jesus, the most profound, and at the same time the most simple and practical teacher the world has ever known, has provided for this need, and has given us a universally applicable test for truth. It is as simple and direct as the acid test for gold. It is the simple question—Does the truth work in our lives? This test is so staggeringly simple that most clever people have passed it over. Truth heals the body, purifies the soul, reforms the sinner, solves difficulties, pacifies strife. *There is no such thing as undemonstrated understanding.* If you wish to know how you really stand spiritually, look about you at your environment, beginning with the body. There can be nothing in the soul that is not demonstrated sooner or later in the outer, and there can be nothing in the outer that does not find some correspondence in the inner. *By their fruits ye shall know them* (Matthew 7:20).

Read Matthew 7:21–23.

We are all willing to do God's will sometimes and in some things, but until there is a complete dedication of one's whole self, there cannot be a complete demonstration. "There is no home for the soul in which there dwells the shadow of an untruth," said George Meredith.

Never is it more true than in the life of the soul that the price of liberty is eternal vigilance. We must not allow any consideration whatever, any institution, any organization, any book, or any man or woman, to come between us and our direct seeking for God. Centers, churches, schools, all fill a useful purpose in providing the physical framework for the distribution of right knowledge, but the actual work must be done by the individual.

Not every one that saith unto me, Lord, Lord, shall enter into the kingdom of heaven; but he that doeth the will of my Father which is in heaven (Matthew 7:21).

Read Matthew 7:24–27.

Therefore whosoever heareth these sayings of mine, and doeth them, I will liken him unto a wise man, which built his house upon a rock (Matthew 7:24).

One of the oldest symbols for the human soul is that of a building, sometimes a dwelling house, and sometimes a temple. The first thing that has to be done by the builder of a house is to select a sound foundation. On the shifting sands of the desert it is impossible to build anything at all, and so when the desert dweller intends to put up a permanent structure he looks about for a rock. Now the Rock is one of the Bible terms for the Christ, and the implication is very obvious. Christ is the one and only foundation upon which we can build the temple of the regenerated soul with safety. As long as we are depending upon something less than that Rock—upon will power, upon so-called material security, upon the good will of others, or upon our own personal resources—we are building upon sand, and great will be our fall.

And it came to pass, when Jesus had ended these sayings, the people were astonished at his doctrine:

For he taught them as one having authority, and not as the scribes (Matthew 7:28–29).

It is always so. The message of Jesus Christ is utterly revolutionary, for it turns our gaze from the outside to the inside, and from man and his works to God.

He taught as one having authority. The greatest glory of the Spiritual Basis is that you begin to *know*. When you have obtained the smallest demonstration by means of prayer, you have experienced something that never leaves you. You have the witness of Truth within yourself, and this is the only authority worth having.

G*ive unto the Lord the glory due unto his name; worship the Lord in the beauty of holiness* (Psalm 29:2).

God is bigger than any problem.

God in you is greater than any difficulty that you have to meet.

God cares for you more than it is possible for any human being to realize.

God can help you in proportion to the degree in which you worship Him. You worship God by really putting your trust in Him instead of in outer conditions, or in fear, or in depression, or in seeming dangers, and so forth.

You worship God by recognizing His presence everywhere, in all people and conditions that you meet; and by praying regularly.

You pray well when you pray with joy.

Glory ye in his holy name: let the heart of them rejoice that seek the Lord (Psalm 105:3).

When you set out to solve a problem by means of prayer you should take all the ordinary normal steps in addition. Do not simply pray and then sit down and wait for something dramatic to happen. For instance, if you are praying for a position, you should pray for it as well as you know how each day, and then go out and visit agencies or prospective employers, write applications, or insert advertisements in suitable periodicals.

If you want a healing, treat about it in whatever way you usually find to be best and, in addition, take whatever material steps seem to be appropriate.

If your business is not prospering, have a checkup to discover if you are managing it efficiently. If you find weak points, as you almost certainly will, you must correct them forthwith.

We certainly cannot expect to go on breaking the laws of the plane on which we live, and expect prayer to compensate for this foolishness.

Whatsoever thy hand findeth to do, do it with thy might . . . (Ecclesiastes 9:10).

There is one thing that means more to us than all the other things in the world, and that is our search for God and the understanding of His nature. Our aim is to learn the practice of the presence of God. We practice the presence of God by seeing Him everywhere, in all things and in all people.

Some years ago I coined the phrase "mental equivalent." For anything that you want in your life—a healthy body, a satisfactory vocation, friends, opportunities, and above all the understanding of God—you must furnish a mental equivalent. Supply yourself with a mental equivalent, and the thing must come to you.

This expression "mental equivalent" is borrowed from physics and chemistry. We speak of the mechanical equivalent of heat, and engineers constantly have to work out the equivalent of one kind of energy in another kind of energy. They have to find out how much coal will be needed to produce so much electricity, and so on. In like manner there is a mental equivalent of every object or occurrence on the physical plane.

The secret of successful living is to build up the mental equivalent that you want; and to get rid of, to expunge, the mental equivalent that you do not want.

I will meditate in thy precepts, and have respect unto thy ways (Psalm 119:15).

The key to life is to build in the mental equivalents of what you want, and to expunge the equivalents of what you do not want. You build in the mental equivalents by thinking with clearness or definiteness, and interest. Remember *clarity* and *interest;* those are the two poles. If you want to be healthy, happy, prosperous, doing a constructive work, having a continuous understanding of God, you think, feel, and get interested in these ends. What we call "feeling" in connection with thought is really interest. Ninety-nine times in a hundred the reason why Christians do not demonstrate is that they lack feeling in their desires or prayers.

How are you going to expunge the wrong mental equivalents? Suppose you have a mental equivalent of resentment, or of unemployment, or of criticism, or of not understanding God. The only way to expunge a wrong mental equivalent is to supply the opposite. The right thought automatically expunges the wrong thought. If you say: "I am not going to think resentment any more," what are you thinking about except resentment? The key to the management of your thinking, and therefore, the key to the management of your destiny, is to substitute an affirmative thought for a negative thought.

The Lord will perfect that which concerneth me . . . (Psalm 138:8).

What you concentrate upon you bring into your life. Many people fail to concentrate successfully because they think that concentration means will power. They suppose that the harder they press the faster they get through. But that is quite wrong.

Think of the photographic process. The secret of a clear picture lies in *focus.* You focus your camera lens steadily for the necessary length of time. Suppose I want to photograph a vase of flowers. I place them in front of the camera and keep them there. But suppose that after a few moments I snatch away the vase and hold a book in front of the camera, and then snatch that away, and hold up a chair, and then put the flowers back for a few moments. You know what will happen to my photograph. It will be a crazy blur. Is not that what people do to their minds when they cannot keep their thoughts concentrated for any length of time? They think health for a few minutes and then they think sickness or fear. They think prosperity and then they think depression. Is it any wonder that man is so apt to demonstrate the "marred image"?

It is always good to make a practical experiment, so I advise you to take a single problem in your life—and just change your mind concerning your problem and keep it changed for a month, and you will be astonished at the results. If you really do keep your thought changed you will not have to wait a month for results.

. . . *he that shall endure unto the end, the same shall be saved* (Matthew 24:13).

There is an instructive legend of the Middle Ages. It seems that a certain citizen was arrested by one of the barons and shut up in a dungeon by a ferocious looking jailer who carried a great key. The door of his cell shut with a bang. He lay in the dark dungeon for twenty years. Each day the big door would be opened with a great creaking; water and bread would be thrust in and the door closed again.

After twenty years the prisoner decided that he wanted to die but he did not want to commit suicide, so the next day when the jailer came he would attack him, and the jailer would then kill him. In preparation he thought he should examine the door, so he turned the handle, and to his amazement the door opened. He found that there was no lock. He groped along the corridor and felt his way upstairs. At the top of the stairs two soldiers were chatting, and they made no attempt to stop him. He crossed the great yard. There was an armed guard on the drawbridge but paid no attention to him, and he walked out a free man. He went home unmolested. He had been a captive, not of stone and iron, but of false belief. He had only thought he was locked in.

Bring my soul out of prison, that I may praise thy name: the righteous shall compass me about; for thou shalt deal bountifully with me (Psalm 142:7).

Read Exodus 19:6–20:20.

Moses was a man of extraordinary understanding of God and of man. He was also one of the great historical leaders of the human race. He was born in Egypt, which was in those days the most highly civilized country in the world. But at the time, the authorities gave orders to kill the male children of the Israelites, and Moses' mother tried to save his life by placing him in a little basket and hiding it at the river's edge where Pharaoh's daughter could not help but see it when she came to the river to bathe. The sister of Moses was told to hide among the tall reeds to guard the baby. The king's daughter saw this little basket, opened it, and when the child cried, her heart was touched. She looked around, and out came the sister, and you know the rest of the story, how the sister was sent to fetch a woman to take care of the child, and brought Moses' own mother.

Now there is a remarkable text here. Pharaoh's daughter says to the woman:

Take this child away, and nurse it for me, and I will give thee thy wages (Exodus 2:9).

In the Bible sense you are the King's Daughters as soon as you reach out for the Truth. The infant Moses is that higher teaching that draws out your heart. Now, how do we nourish our infant Moses? By prayer and meditation. Otherwise the child will starve. However, if we take the child and nurse it, we shall get our wages, and our wages shall be freedom, peace of mind, harmony, understanding, and the fellowship of God Himself.

*A*nd *God heard their groaning, and God remembered his cove-nant . . . and had respect unto them* (Exodus 2:24–25).

Moses grew up as the adopted son of Pharaoh's daughter with all the privileges and training of royalty. As the years went by and he witnessed the oppression of his people, he determined to lead them out of their bondage into a better life—their Promised Land. We are told "that their cry went up to God" (Exodus 2:24) and God Himself led them safely through their wilderness. Then at the time of their uncertainty, their moral laxness and emotional confusion, He gave Moses certain basic rules of life, which we still know as the Ten Commandments.

The Ten Commandments at their face value are true and valid, but that is only the beginning. If people are going to escape from the continuous strife and struggle of life, they must have something more. So within these commandments he concealed the deeper laws for those who were ready for them. And within those again, he concealed the deepest and highest spiritual teaching for those who were ready for that.

In other words, Moses designed these laws of life so that the higher we go spiritually, or the deeper we go intellectually, the more we can get out of them.

THE FIRST COMMANDMENT

I am the Lord thy God, which have brought thee out of the land of Egypt, out of the house of bondage.

Thou shalt have no other gods before me (Exodus 20:2, 3).

Moses lived in Egypt over three thousand years ago, and he led some six hundred thousand people out of Egypt and through the wilderness. That is historical. But, Moses also stands for a faculty in yourself, and the things that Moses did typify your states of mind.

The mountain means prayer—the elevated consciousness. We are told that the general public were not allowed to go up Mount Sinai, but that does not mean that certain people were not good enough to go up. It means that if we want to go up the mountain—if we want to raise our consciousness, if we want to get closer to God— we must prepare ourselves by prayer. If we want to go up the mountain, we have to become a high priest spiritually and we must rid ourselves of our faults and weaknesses—otherwise we cannot elevate our consciousness and get our contact with God.

Moses had his revelation, and then he realized it as the experience that God and man are one. When he got that revelation, Moses brought back the laws of life, beginning with the First Commandment, as we call it.

What is the beginning of the First Commandment? *I am the Lord thy God.* Our trouble in our religious life nearly always is that we think, "In the beginning Me." That is very human but it does not get us the revelation that Moses got. After affirming *I am the Lord thy God . . .* the First Commandment says *thou shalt have no other gods before me.*

THE SECOND COMMANDMENT

Read Exodus 20:4–6.

Thou shalt not take unto thee any graven image . . . (Exodus 20:4).

A primitive people needed to be thus instructed because they were much given to making idols of a palpable sort. We do not do these things, but whenever we give power to anything but God, we are making that thing into a graven image. For example, we give power to our ailments, particularly if it is a favorite ailment. We all know people who say, "My rheumatism," and they say it quite lovingly. Been with them a long time! Has become a conversation piece! Others say, "My indigestion." We are making a graven image of these things. It is only when we take power away from them that we can heal them.

If you forget God and worship graven images of any kind, you are going to suffer. You can demolish a stone statue; you can burn a wooden one. The way to destroy mental images is to stop thinking of them and giving them power.

This commandment goes on to say, "For I the Lord thy God am a jealous God." Moses does not mean that God is jealous like a man, but that God must have first place. The trouble with many pious people is that they want God to be vice-president, keeping the presidency for themselves. So the Bible uses the word "jealous" in the sense that if you give power to anything but God, you have lost God altogether. You cannot have a percentage of God. Either God is the only power, or nothing at all.

THE THIRD COMMANDMENT

Thou shalt not take the name of the Lord thy God in vain; for the Lord will not hold him guiltless that taketh his name in vain (Exodus 20:7).

Now this law of life really means you cannot take the name of the Lord in vain. If you try to do so you will fail because when you take the name of God unto yourself and implement it, then consequences will follow. It is a pity more of us do not realize that fact because constantly we are trying to take the name of the Lord in vain. The name of God is your conviction concerning God. Your idea of God will determine your whole life. If you believe that God is good, God is love, God has all power, God is intelligence, all the conditions of your life will steadily improve. If you believe God is intelligent but not good—I know people would not dare to say that, but people who think that God sends sickness and trouble really believe in a God who is not good—if you believe in a God who has all intelligence, but is not loving, then your idea of the nature of God must work out. Troubles will come to you, and you will not overcome them because you are saying, "God sent this trouble for a good purpose, and I must put up with it." You will put up with it. Your idea of God cannot be in vain. It will work out for you in accordance with your belief.

There is no one of us who is not limiting God in some respect in his thought and because of that we are going to suffer limitation in some way, for we cannot take the name of God in vain.

THE FOURTH COMMANDMENT

Read Exodus 20:8–11.

Remember the sabbath day, to keep it holy (Exodus 20:8).

This commandment about the Sabbath Day was given to the people at the time of their leaving Egypt and going into the desert, and on the surface it meant what it said for that age. It was a wonderful thing in Moses' day to insist that everybody set aside one day a week to think about God or at least to oblige him to stop his secular activities. No rule can make a man religious, or give him faith, but it can help.

Like all the other commandments, this one is instruction in seeking the presence of God everywhere, particularly where the trouble seems to be. Where there is fear and doubt He brings faith, where there is lack He brings abundance.

But here in this commandment about the Sabbath Day there is a still deeper meaning. When you are praying every day and recognizing that God is working in you and in all your affairs, there will be a sense in which every day will be a Sabbath, because for you every day will be a holy day. One of the most wonderful things about the Bible teaching is that we get rid of the distinction between the sacred and the secular. That is one of the most important steps in the whole history of the soul.

God is present everywhere. For those who understand Jesus' teaching, it is always the Sabbath Day, and the place whereon they stand is holy ground.

THE FIFTH COMMANDMENT

Honour thy father and thy mother: that thy days may be long upon the land which the Lord thy God giveth thee (Exodus 20:12).

We should respect our parents just because they are our parents, but that teaching is just the very outer layer of this commandment. Underneath it is instruction in divine metaphysics because your real father and mother is God. When this commandment says, "Honour thy father and thy mother," it brings in the two poles, the male and the female, and, of course, polarity is the motive power of the universe. In the Bible, mother means the feeling nature, and the father is the knowledge nature. Most people have one side or the other more developed. When our prayers fail and we do not demonstrate, we fail because we are not honoring our father and our mother.

THE SIXTH COMMANDMENT

Thou shalt not kill (Exodus 20:13).

As rules of conduct, the commandments are just such "thou shalt nots" as you see written up, "No smoking" or "No thoroughfare." But when you get behind the surface meaning, then "Thou shalt not" becomes "Thou canst not."

So this commandment, "Thou shalt not kill," is fundamentally an expression of the cosmic law that you cannot kill, and the sooner you find that out the better. We are always trying to kill. However, this commandment is here to tell us that to think we can kill anything is to lay up trouble for ourselves that will have to be met and wiped out some time or other.

Nothing ever dies from the outside. No one can kill your character. No one can kill your peace of mind. No one can kill your business, or your reputation, or anything that is yours. You can, but nobody else can. No man or woman was ever yet destroyed from the outside.

Many people waste their lives in thinking how they are being hurt, or damaged, or injured by other people; how good they could be, what marvelous things they could do, if it were not for others. So long as you believe that, you cannot progress. As soon as you know that nobody can hurt you, then you are free to overtake any mistakes, and to be and do the thing you want.

THE SEVENTH COMMANDMENT

Thou shalt not commit adultery (Exodus 20:14).

Naturally, this commandment means what it says. The Christian standard of conduct with regard to personal purity will never be improved on. Not to commit adultery is fundamentally important because on it is founded the sanctity of the family. But, of course, there is a great deal more in it than that.

One of the most common Hebrew synonyms was adultery for idolatry. In the Old Testament these two words are almost always interchangeable. The worship of false gods was described as adultery. The fundamental idea behind this commandment is to have one God. As you read through the Old Testament, you will find that the idea of the adulterous woman who is unfaithful to her husband constantly means the human soul that is turning away to some other god.

THE EIGHTH COMMANDMENT

Thou shalt not steal (Exodus 20:15).

Many people will say, "We always knew that we must not steal. If we do we shall have trouble and probably wind up in prison." All through the ages it is only the smallest percentage of human beings who have stolen. Respect for other people's property was learned early in the history of civilization. However, this most fundamental law of life means that actually we cannot steal. You may say you know someone who broke into your house and took your silver. The burglar who took your silver actually transferred some silver from your house to someone else's house, but did he get away with it? If that silver belonged to you by right of consciousness, all the burglars in the world could not have taken it away. In fact, if you had this understanding, you could take a ten dollar bill, put it on the sidewalk in Times Square, and return the next day and it would still be there. Your consciousness of the presence of God in other people would have been so strong that no one could have taken from you what belonged to you by right of that consciousness.

These ten laws of life are things that cannot be done, and so, says the great prophet in effect, do not waste yourself or your life trying to do these things. They cannot be done. They conflict with the fundamental Law of Being.

When we give up trying to steal, then we shall begin to have our own. We shall come into our own rights, and when we get that, liberation will not be very far off.

THE NINTH COMMANDMENT

Thou shalt not bear false witness against thy neighbour (Exodus 20:16).

First, the obvious meaning is very important although it is only the beginning—do not tell lies about people.

We have to apply this principle of not bearing false witness right throughout our lives. It is very important to practice because whatever you say about another person will happen to you, yourself. If you lie about another person—that is an unpleasant word but I am using it because it is the right word—someone will lie about you. Jesus says so in the seventh chapter of Matthew, verses one and two:

Judge not, that ye be not judged.

For with what judgment ye judge, ye shall be judged: and with what measure ye mete, it shall be measured to you again.

However, the fundamental meaning of this commandment, "Thou shalt not bear false witness," is that you always express what you are. You cannot be one thing and express another. Emerson says, "What you are shouts so loudly that I cannot hear what you say." We are always witnessing to what we are. So again, "Thou shalt not" really means "You cannot"—you cannot permanently bear false witness.

The true witness is the full expression of God's man. You will be bearing true witness to your neighbor when you are regenerated in soul. What does regeneration mean? It means the building of a new soul, not correcting the old one. When you change the soul, automatically the flesh changes, the skin changes, the blood vessels and the nerves and the bones change. But regeneration must begin with a change in the soul, not with anything in the outer world.

When we really *know* these things, we shall be bearing true witness.

THE TENTH COMMANDMENT

Thou shalt not covet . . . any thing that is thy neighbour's (Exodus 20:17).

There are several phrases concerning coveting. You are not to covet your neighbor's house, nor his wife, nor his manservant, nor his maidservant, nor his cattle, nor anything that is his. Much of the evil in the world is caused by wanting something to which one is not entitled. Moses knew what covetousness does to us in what we call today the unconscious or the subconscious.

Coveting affects the soul of man. Even if your coveting never leads you to take anything that does not belong to you, it undermines and ultimately rots your soul. It shuts you off from God. Why? Because to covet something means that you do not understand the Law of Being. You do not understand that whatever you are getting or lacking is the outpicturing and expression of your consciousness. Until you understand that you cannot be saved.

There is not anything in the world that you ever conceived of that God has not got in abundance. God's supply is infinite, and to envy someone else because he seems to have more is to deny your own contact with God.

And . . . *there were thunders and lightnings, and a thick cloud* . . . (Exodus 19:16).

These are dramatic expressions of the change of consciousness as we move away from the common things of life to the higher things.

In these days of the Exodus, the conditions of the outer world answered very quickly to man's thoughts because people believed it was possible. Moses took his people across the Red Sea by the power of thought, and he was able to do that because in those days people believed in the power of thought. They believed that God could take them across the Red Sea dry shod, and He did.

Moses had the true knowledge of God from his father's people, the Hebrews. It was the historical mission of the Hebrews to teach that God is not a limited, corporeal being, but incorporeal, infinite, divine mind.

Moses saw clearly the unity of God and man, and the unity of man and man. He got more than a flash of what we call the cosmic consciousness. That was his illumination. Then he realized that he must give this to humanity.

Why not organize the business of living in a big way? Why creep along, as some people do, from one tiny stepping stone to another, instead of striding out boldly? Why be content with poor health, uninteresting work, or restricted conditions, when many other people have already risen above these things?

There is a way out of limitation that never fails. It is this, take God for your partner. If you will really make God your business partner in every department of your life, you will be amazed at the quick and striking results that you will obtain. Of course, if you want God to be your partner, you will have to include Him in every corner and every phase of your life.

Most people would be thrilled to be able to go into partnership with some great industrial or financial magnate; they would feel that their future was assured. But here is a partnership with Infinite Wisdom and Infinite Power awaiting you.

I am the vine, ye are the branches: He that abideth in me, and I in him, the same bringeth forth much fruit: for without me ye can do nothing (John 15:5).

The Ninety-first Psalm is one of the greatest chapters in the Bible. Like the rest of Scripture, the underlying thought is developed through a series of symbols, and it is by the appreciation of the values lying behind these symbols that the power of this prayer is appropriated.

The way to get the most out of this psalm is to read it through quietly; pausing after each clause to consider the meaning and assenting to this mentally. If you are fearful you will find, after working through the prayer two or three times, that your fear will have gone and that you are now looking at things from a different point of view.

He that dwelleth in the secret place of the most High shall abide under the shadow of the Almighty (Psalm 91:1).

The Secret Place of the most High is your own consciousness, and this fact is the most important practical discovery in the science of religion. The error usually made is to suppose the Secret Place of the most High to be somewhere outside of yourself, an error fatal to our hopes, because our success in prayer depends upon getting some degree of contact with God; and since He is only to be contacted within, as long as we are looking without we must fail in our objective. Jesus emphasized this truth, *The kingdom of God is within you.* Again he said that when we pray we are to enter into the closet and shut the door, meaning, to retire in thought within our own consciousness. In fact, this doctrine of the Secret Place and the wonders that can happen therein is taught throughout the Bible.

To abide under the shadow of the Almighty means to live under the protection of God Himself. Eastern people, and especially those with a desert background, such as the people of Palestine, look upon the sun as a danger, even an enemy, from which they need to be safeguarded. Shade is sanctuary, or safety—"the shadow of a mighty rock in a weary land." The exhausted traveler sinks down in the shade for his long-sought rest.

God is called "The Almighty" in order to impress us with the fact that He really is All-mighty, and can therefore overcome our present difficulty, no matter how big it may seem.

. . . *for with God all things are possible* (Mark 10:27).

Consider, however, that the promise is made to "him that dwelleth." If we only run into the Secret Place now and again, we can scarcely be said to dwell there. God will come to our rescue whenever we pray, but if we seldom think of Him, we may experience difficulty in making our contact in an emergency. By means of daily meditation we dwell in the Secret Place.

R̲ead Psalm 91.

Observe that the poem opens by announcing the irresistible power of prayer. Then in order to bring home the fact that this law applies to us, and that by no possibility could we be an exception, it now changes over to the first person and makes us say "I." It compels us to voice the I AM.

I will say of the Lord, He is my refuge and my fortress: my God; in him will I trust. The Lord means God. How can knowledge be a presence? Secular knowledge, which is intellectual, cannot; but the true knowledge of God is an actual experience—not a thing of the head, but of the heart—and this is indeed a Presence. As a general rule, people contact this Real Self only vaguely and occasionally. Then, if they pray regularly, the gleams of intuition gradually strengthen into a definite sense of the Presence of God.

In Him will I trust. However worried or depressed you may be, however full of doubts and misgivings, still the fact that you are praying means that you have at least enough faith for that. The faith to go on praying in the midst of doubts about results is the tiny grain of mustard seed that Jesus says is sufficient for practical purposes. Declaring *in Him will I trust* means that you have now determined to trust by ceasing to worry and fear. This is the legitimate and spiritual use of the will.

Read Psalm 91.

And now the Word of Truth is represented as addressing you with an authoritative assurance that your prayer will be answered, that in some way or other—not necessarily in the way that you expect—you will be rescued from your difficulty.

Surely He shall deliver thee from the snare of the fowler, and from the noisome pestilence. He shall cover thee with His feathers, and under His wings shalt thou trust: His Truth shall be thy shield and buckler. You are to have no apprehension, for your protection is now assured in one of those illustrations from everyday life in which the Bible abounds. The motherly hen, at the slightest threat of danger, gathers the little chicks under her wings, covering them "with her feathers"; thus does God shield you from all danger once you have elected to trust Him. *His truth shall be thy shield and buckler.* It is the knowledge of the Truth about God and man that makes the demonstration.

Thou shalt not be afraid for the terror by night; nor for the arrow that flieth by day; nor for the pestilence that walketh in darkness; nor for the destruction that wasteth at noonday. The arrow that flieth by day and the destruction that wasteth at noon refer to any difficulty of which you are consciously aware. It is, so to say, a daytime problem. The terror by night and the pestilence that walketh in darkness, on the contrary, imply something that, unknown to you, is working in your subconscious mind. Modern psychology has shown that most of our difficulties have their roots in the depth of the subconscious. These are indeed terrors of the mental night and pestilences of the darkness.

Read Psalm 91.

A thousand shall fall at thy side, and ten thousand at thy right hand; but it shall not come nigh thee. Only with thine eyes shalt thou behold and see the reward of the wicked. This clause has been taken to indicate some kind of favoritism on the part of God, whereas, of course, such a thing is impossible. It means simply that those who pray are saved from trouble that would otherwise overtake them, and that does, in fact, overtake those who do not pray.

Because thou hast made the Lord, which is my refuge, even the most High, thy habitation; There shall no evil befall thee, neither shall any plague come nigh thy dwelling. In the Bible, the word *promise* is the name given to a statement of some spiritual law. So, a "Bible promise" is a statement of the consequences that naturally follow from certain states of consciousness. If Boyle's law were written in the Bible idiom, it would read something like this: "As I live, saith the Lord, whenever thou shalt double the pressure of a gas, thou shalt halve the volume, temperature remaining constant." In the language of natural science, our Bible promise would run: "By meditating regularly on the Presence of God with you, and directing your life in accordance with that fact, you become immune from any kind of danger."

Read Psalm 91.

For He shall give His angels charge over thee, to keep thee in all thy ways. They shall bear thee up in their hands, lest thou dash thy foot against a stone. This is one of the loveliest of all the promises in the Bible. For tender beauty it stands alone. *He shall give His angels charge over thee, to keep thee in all thy ways*—and it is meant for you and for me. It might have seemed appropriate enough that some exalted Being should be given an escort of angels to surround him, to support him, to keep him in all his ways. But the Bible is the book of Everyman, and this promise is given to you and to me.

Read Psalm 91.

Thou shalt tread upon the lion and adder: the young lion and the dragon shalt thou trample under feet.

Here the lion stands for a difficulty of which we are so afraid that it seems to us a very lion in our path, rushing at us in the open. How different, on the other hand, is the attack of the adder, or snake; for it creeps upon us in the dark. And here we are promised that our complexes, dragons though they be, shall be dissolved by the realization of God. There is nothing that can be done by any form of psychotherapy that cannot be better done by the Practice of the Presence of God.

The last three verses are in themselves a glorious psalm of ringing joy and triumph.

Because he hath set his love upon me, therefore will I deliver him. There is nothing hypothetical or contingent here. The statement indicates the fixed decision—*I will deliver him.* And why?—*because he has set his love upon me.*

I will set him on high, because he hath known my name. In the Bible the "name" of anything means the nature or character of that thing. Now the nature of God is perfect, omnipresent, all-powerful good, boundless love; and to "know" this is to be set on hand above all our difficulties.

The last two verses gather up all the implications and promises of this wonderful poem, and present them to the fearful or doubting heart as a song of triumph. *He shall call upon me, and I will answer him: I will be with him in trouble; I will deliver him, and honour him. With long life will I satisfy him, and show him my salvation.*

We make spiritual progress by putting God into every corner of our lives. Most people on the spiritual path are willing to give God a generous portion of their lives, but there is often one little corner where they do not wish the divine Light to shine.

Bluebeard, you remember, kept open house, with the exception of one little room—and there he drew the line. His current wife, or any of the neighbors could go all over the premises and welcome, until they came to that one little room, the Bluebeard chamber, that was forbidden. Yet that one little locked-up room contained the tragedy of the house.

The contents of the Bluebeard room need not be anything that we usually call horrible. There may just be selfishness, laziness, spiritual pride, or any of the more "respectable" but very deadly sins. There may be an old grudge or bitter remorse.

Open every door of your soul to God. Have no place where the light of His presence does not shine.

The secret things belong unto the Lord our God . . . (Deuteronomy 29:29).

God's time for your demonstration is now. The time God wants you to be healed is *now*. The time God wants you to be in your true place is *now*. The Bible says that the day of salvation is *now*.

God is ready the moment you are. There is nothing to wait for except the changing of your own consciousness. People often make the mistake of saying, "I know my demonstration will come at the right time." But the only time to be harmonious and satisfied is now. The time to be happy is now and the place is here. Did not Jesus say, *The kingdom of heaven is at hand,* and by this he meant close by.

Do not keep yourself out of the Kingdom of Heaven by inventing postponements, but change your consciousness now, for it can all happen in a moment.

. . . *that now it is high time to awake out of sleep: for now is our salvation nearer than when we believed* (Romans 13:11).

You are continually "treating" your conditions with the thoughts that you hold concerning them. What you really think about anything, is your "treatment" of that thing. Many people have the idea that they are only "treating" when they call it "treating," but no matter what you call it, your thought concerning any subject is a treatment. This is the reason visible conditions are always the expression of invisible thought.

If you will begin systematically to treat every side of your life with a series of positive, correct thoughts, and keep to this practice for even a few weeks, you will be amazed to find how much everything will change for the better.

. . . be ye transformed by the renewing of your mind . . . (Romans 12:2).

Your destiny depends entirely upon your own mental conduct. You may think that you know this already, but if you do not act upon it, it is certain that you do not really know it. Most people would be amazed to discover how much negative thinking they indulge in. Thought is so swift and habit is so strong that unless you are very careful you will constantly transgress.

Suppose that, quite without your knowledge, an invisible dictaphone were strapped on your shoulders the first thing tomorrow morning, and that you carried it about all day until the last thing tomorrow night. Then suppose that this record were played over to you so that every word you had uttered for a whole day was repeated to you. Well, if you are an average human being you would probably be embarrassed. Yet it really does happen that everything we say, and think and do, is recorded—in the subconscious mind—and our daily experience is simply that record being played over to us by the Law of Being.

Never forget that the circumstances of your life tomorrow are molded by your mental conduct of today.

I have chosen the way of truth . . . (Psalm 119:30).

There is no need to be unhappy. There is no need to be disappointed, or oppressed, or aggrieved. There is no need for illness or failure or discouragement. There is no necessity for anything but an abounding interest and joy in life.

As long as you accept a negative condition at its own valuation, so long will you remain in bondage to it; but you have only to assert your birthright as a free man or woman and you will be free.

Success and happiness are the natural conditions of mankind. It is actually easier to demonstrate these things than the reverse. Bad habits of thinking and acting may obscure this fact for a time, just as a wrong way of walking or sitting, or holding a pen or a musical instrument may seem to be easier than the proper way, because we have accustomed ourselves to it; but the proper way is the easier nevertheless.

Unhappiness, frustration, poverty, loneliness are really bad habits that their victims have become accustomed to bear, believing that there is no way out, whereas there is a way; and that way is simply to acquire good habits of working with the Law instead of against it.

Open thou mine eyes, that I may behold wondrous things out of thy Law (Psalm 119:18).

In the depths of his being man always feels intuitively that there is a way out of his difficulties if only he can find it. The infant, as yet uncontaminated by the defeatism of his elders, simply refuses to tolerate inharmony on any terms, and therefore he demonstrates over it. When he is hungry he tells the world while many a sophisticated adult goes without. Does he find a pin sticking in some part of his anatomy? Not for him a sigh of resignation to the supposed "will of God," or a whine about never having any luck, or a sigh that what cannot be cured must be endured. His instincts tell him that life and harmony are inseparable.

Refuse to tolerate anything less than harmony. You can have a happy and joyous life. But to do so you must seize the rudder of your own destiny and steer boldly for the port that you intend to make. What are you *doing* about your future?

For not the hearers of the law are just before God, but the doers of the law shall be justified (Romans 2:13).

Read Revelation 6.

The Four Horsemen of the Apocalypse give the key to the nature of man as we know him. When you understand these symbols thoroughly you will understand your own makeup, and you will be able to begin the work of getting dominion over yourself and your surroundings.

The Bible is not written in the style of a modern book. It has a method of its own of conveying knowledge through picturesque symbols, the reason being that this is the only possible way in which knowledge could be given to people in all ages in different parts of the world and of different degrees of spiritual development. A symbol appeals to any audience, each individual getting just what he is ready for.

The Four Horsemen of the Apocalypse stand for the four parts or elements of our human nature. There is, first of all, the physical body—the thing that you see when you look into the glass. Then there is your feeling nature or emotions, and although you cannot "see" your feelings, you are tremendously conscious of them. Third, there is your intellect, which contains every bit of knowledge that you possess. Finally, there is your spiritual nature, your real eternal self; the true you, the I AM, the Indwelling Christ. This is your real identity, which is eternal. Almost everyone believes in its existence, but most people are very little conscious of it as an actuality.

Ultimately the time will come when the first three will be merged in the fourth, and then we shall all know instead of only *believing* that the spiritual nature is all.

And ye shall seek me, and find me, when ye shall search for me with all your heart (Jeremiah 29:13).

And *I looked, and behold a pale horse: and his name that sat on him was Death, and Hell followed with him* (Revelation 6:8).

The first horse is the Pale Horse and "pale" means the color of terror, a kind of ashen gray. The Pale Horse stands for the physical body. If you live but for the body, there is nothing but hell awaiting you on this plane or anywhere else. The body is the most cruel taskmaster of all, when it is allowed to be the ruler. The Pale Horse indicates all other physical addictions too—what the Bible sometimes calls the "world"—money, position, material honors. Whoever lives for worldly pursuits, is the rider on the Pale Horse.

And there went out another horse that was red: and power was given to him that sat thereon to take peace from the earth (Revelation 6:4).

The Red Horse is your emotional nature, your feelings. It is dangerous to allow your emotions to have control. This does not mean that emotion is a bad thing in itself. Uncontrolled emotion is a bad thing. A strong emotional nature is a splendid endowment if you are the master, but if it is mastering you, you are riding the Red Horse.

. . . And I beheld, and lo a black horse; and he that sat on him had a pair of balances in his hand (Revelation 6:5).

A pair of scales is here a symbol of unbalance. The Black Horse stands for the intellect. Riding the Black Horse is letting your intellect dominate to the exclusion of the emotional, and especially of the spiritual, nature. It is a good thing to have the intellect well trained, but it is a misfortune to let it be the master. Western civilization has been definitely riding the Black Horse since the close of the Middle Ages. Humanity has developed scientific, intellectual knowledge far beyond the point to which it has developed the moral and spiritual understanding of the race.

And I saw, and behold a white horse: and he that sat on him had a bow; and a crown was given unto him: and he went forth conquering, and to conquer (Revelation 6:2).

The White Horse is the spiritual nature, and the man or woman who rides the White Horse achieves freedom, and joy, and ultimate happiness and harmony.

We are told two very interesting things about the Horseman on the White Horse: the Bible says that he that sat on him had a bow. The bow and arrow is an ancient symbol of the spoken Word. When you speak the Word you shoot an arrow. It goes where you aim it. The Horseman on the White Horse speaks the Word. The rider on the White Horse also wears a crown, and the crown is a symbol of victory. The rider on the White Horse is always the victor.

This, then, is the story of the Four Horsemen of the Apocalypse. If you want peace, an understanding of God, there is only one way— *you must ride the White Horse.*

Genesis means origin or beginning, and this, the first book of the Bible, explains how things and conditions come into existence. Genesis deals with this creative power of thought. The first section deals with generic thought. The second, the story of Adam and Eve, deals with specific thought, or how a given person builds every condition that exists in his life. The sections concerning Cain and Abel, the tower of Babel, the flood, the story of Abraham and his family, the story of Joseph and his brethren, all deal in different ways with the creative power of thought, showing how it is the genesis of all things that exist. The book of Genesis is partly allegorical and partly historical. Unless you have the spiritual meaning behind the story, you do not possess the Bible at all.

The covenant of Sinai, necessary and good in its place, signifies the attempt to order things from the outside and is, of course, much better than anarchy; but he who is on the spiritual path must pass beyond this to the spiritual Jerusalem, which is the ordering of things from the inside by the Practice of the Presence of God. This is the new Jerusalem that cometh straight down from God out of heaven.

And I John saw the holy city, new Jerusalem, coming down from God out of heaven . . . (Revelation 21:2).

The book of Genesis having explained the creative power of thought, the other books of the Bible then proceed to illustrate the way in which the laws of thought work in different circumstances, but Genesis is the foundation of it all.

And *the whole earth was of one language, and of one speech* (Genesis 11:1).

Read Genesis 11:1–9.

The story of the tower of Babel is so simple, so concrete, and so clear, that if you only heard it once when you were a child you could never forget it. It is, of course, a parable. The word *Babel* means confusion and this parable teaches that when you deny the omnipotence of God, and you do this whenever you give power to anything else, only confusion can follow. To be guilty of that sin is really to have many gods, and that was the characteristic fault of the heathen. Those who knew the truth about God worshiped Him and Him alone, and they received the protection and the inspiration that only the Truth can give. At times, however, many of those who had known the Truth, forgot it for a season, and inevitably things began to go wrong.

If you should be in difficulties of any kind, it is certain that you have been committing the sin of the heathen in some way; it may be that at some point you have seen the higher and deliberately chosen the lower. Now, if you will turn back to God once more, and reaffirm your faith in Him, all will be well again.

The story of the tower of Babel begins by saying that the whole earth was of one language, and of one speech. That is to say, there was unity of thought and expression. Your faith was firm and dynamic. Then you allowed your consciousness to fall. *And it came to pass, as they journeyed from the east, that they found a plain in the land of Shinar; and they dwelt there* (Genesis 11:2). The plain means any kind of negative thinking in contradistinction to the hill or mountain, which stands for prayer or spiritual insight. The Bible mentions that they *dwelt* on that plain (or in that state of mind). It is not an occasional negative thought that does the harm, it is the thought or the false belief that is dwelt upon that causes your trouble.

Habitual wrong thinking, false beliefs, long entertained, build up a conviction both conscious and subconscious that we have to rely upon ourselves. Of course, nothing could be more discouraging than such an idea, and in its turn it produces more fear.

In the parable these people got the absurd idea that they could reach Heaven (regain harmony) by building a material tower. This describes that sense of insecurity and apprehension that has always beset the greater part of mankind because they have not realized the Presence and Power of God, and their essential unity with Him.

Then the account says that the Lord scattered the people abroad, and confounded their language so that they could not understand one another's speech. The confusion of tongues is a graphic description of the state of mind of those who have not yet begun to center their lives on God, for only fear and chaos can come to them until they do.

Read 1 Corinthians 13.

Divine Love never fails. Divine Love solves every problem. Statements like these appear again and again in metaphysical books, and, of course, they are perfectly true; certain it is that many people firmly believe them, and yet have obviously been unable to prove them in demonstration. Why is this?

The explanation is that, consciously or unconsciously, people think of Love as some sort of Power outside of themselves; and they expect that presently, if they beg hard enough, this Power will come down and rescue them. There is, in fact, no such outside power, and therefore you cannot receive help in that way. The only place where Love can exist, as far as you are concerned, is in your own heart. Any love that is not in your heart does not exist for you.

The thing for you to do, then, is to fill your own heart with Love, by thinking it, feeling it, and expressing it; and when this sense of Love is vivid enough it will heal you and solve your problems, and it will enable you to heal others too. That is the Law of Being and none of us can change it.

Yea, I have loved thee with an everlasting love . . . (Jeremiah 31:3).

The old adage, "An ounce of prevention is worth a pound of cure," is just as true in the spiritual life as it is in the material world. A great many people wait to make their contact with God until a serious difficulty is upon them and then they hasten to find a spiritual solution. Of course, it is better to seek God under such circumstances than never to find Him at all. But why wait for trouble? Many a difficulty could be prevented or lightened if we were to make our contact with God now.

The Bible says now is the day of salvation. Now is the accepted time.

If you will put your life in God's hands now through daily prayer and meditation and complete willingness to do His will, you will find that your problems will grow less as time goes on, and you will have acquired that serenity and poise that only God can give. Then, come what may, nothing shall disturb you.

And now, Lord, what wait I for? my hope is in thee (Psalm 39:7).

As children of the Most High we have a divine heritage and therefore a right to expect that God will take care of us in every way. The Bible is full of promises as to what God will do for His children, but perhaps Jesus put it the most plainly when he said,

What man is there of you, whom if his son ask bread, will he give him a stone?

Or if he ask a fish, will he give him a serpent?

If ye then, being evil, know how to give good gifts unto your children, how much more shall your Father which is in heaven give good things to them that ask him? (Matthew 7:9–11).

So you have a divine right to expect all these good things from God. But what does God expect of us? Well, God has a right to expect that we will put Him first in our hearts. Then God expects us to have a lively faith. Faith in itself is a reliance upon the goodness of God.

And lastly, God expects us to go to Him in prayer—as a son who knows that even before he has asked, the loving Father has answered.

Most hotel rooms are furnished with a notice that says "do not disturb." The guest has only to hang this outside the door and he can sleep in peace as long as he wishes. Some people appear to have hung such a notice on their brains; they deeply resent anything like a new idea, or even a new and better way of considering familiar things. They are slumbering away their lives in a kind of semi-coma; repeating mechanically the time-worn phrases and threadbare ideas of the past. *Not dead, but sleepeth,* might very well be said of them, and, indeed, their consciousness is a mental cemetery.

If you have been sleeping like this, pull yourself together, rub the mental sleep from your eyes. Now is the day of salvation. Start right in today to handle at least one important part of your life in a new way. Break at least one rusty fetter today, and once this process begins you will be astonished to find how far you will go, and what wonderful things you will attain to.

Awake thou that sleepest, and arise from the dead, and Christ shall give thee light (Ephesians 5:14).

The world is not going to the dogs. The human race is not doomed. Civilization is not going to crash. The captain is on the bridge. Humanity is going through a difficult time, but humanity has gone through difficulties many times before in its long history, and has always come through, strengthened and purified.

Do not worry yourself about the universe collapsing. It is not going to collapse, and anyway that question is none of your business. The captain is on the bridge. If the survival of humanity depended upon you or me, it would be a poor lookout for the Great Enterprise, would it not?

The captain is on the bridge. God is still in business. All that you have to do is to realize the Presence of God where trouble seems to be, to do your nearest duty to the very best of your ability; and to keep an even mind until the storm is over.

Great peace have they which love thy law: and nothing shall offend them (Psalm 119:165).

Shallow thinkers sometimes say doggedly and pessimistically, "Human nature never changes," or, "You can't change human nature." The truth is that there is no need for human nature to change. The nature of man is such that he can bring an unlimited quantity of good into his life. That is his nature, and no better arrangement could be imagined.

Human nature is such that man can turn to God anywhere at any time, and by believing in His care and protection, and thinking in accordance with this belief, fill his heart with peace and poise, rebuild his body into health and strength, and surround himself with harmonious and joyous conditions.

I am come that they might have life, and that they might have it more abundantly (John 10:10).

Don't be a grave robber. Let corpses alone. In due course nature disposes of such remains, if they are left undisturbed. Every time you dig up an old grievance or an old mistake by rehearsing it in your mind or, still worse, by telling someone else about it, you are simply ripping open a grave—and you know what you may expect to find.

Live the present. Prepare intelligently for the future—and let the past alone. This is what Jesus meant when he said, . . . *let the dead bury their dead* (Matthew 8:22).

Make a law for yourself today that you are not going to touch mentally any negative thing that has happened up to the present moment—and keep that law. Life is too precious for grave robbing. The past is past—liquidate it. If a negative memory comes into your mind, cremate it with the right thought (the fire of Love) and forget it.

As long as we insist upon telling God His business, nothing very much can come of our prayers.

The ox, the mule, the donkey, will obediently pull your plow and your cart, and take them where you want to go; but you have to know where that is, and how to get there. The unicorn will not do chores. He will not pull a cart or turn a mill. He will not take orders. The unicorn knows where he is going, and it is always somewhere that you could not choose because you never heard of it; and in your present consciousness you could not even dream that such a place could exist.

Nevertheless, there are such places, and the unicorn knows them, and is not interested in anything less. Some day it may happen, probably when you least expect it, that the unicorn will suddenly appear at your side, eyes flashing, nostrils quivering, pawing the ground with impatience. When that happens, do not try to put a bridle on him, or to look for some task for him to do. He will not do it, and there will not be time. No sooner, seemingly, has he appeared than off he will go again. So do not pause, but leap upon his back, for he is a flying steed, and he wings his way to the gates of the morning.

On that ride problems are not solved—*they disappear.*

Will the unicorn be willing to serve thee, or abide by thy crib? Canst thou bind the unicorn with his band in the furrow? or will he harrow the valleys after thee? (Job 39:9–10).

FEAR

The Bible says that the fear of the Lord is the beginning of wisdom, and the beginning of knowledge. This has misled many people, because the truth is that fear is entirely evil and is indeed the only enemy we have. You can heal any condition if you can get rid of the fear attaching to it. Trouble or sickness is nothing but subconscious fear outpictured in our surroundings. It is true at all times that "we have nothing to fear but fear."

How then do we account for the texts quoted? The answer is that in the Bible the fear of God means reverence for God, not fear in the usual sense of the word. Reverence for God is the beginning of wisdom. How do we show reverence for God? By seeing God everywhere, refusing to recognize anything unlike Him, and by living the Christ life.

Confidence is worship. You worship whatever you trust. Are you trusting more in fear or in God? What are you worshiping? That is the test.

Acquaint now thyself with him, and be at peace (Job 22:21).

SALVATION

The word *salvation* appears more than 120 times in the Bible. It was in constant use among religious people of past generations, and while it is not so often heard today, the fact remains that it is one of the most important words in the Bible and among the least well understood.

The word *salvation* in the Bible means perfect health, harmony, and freedom. These things are the will of God for man—for you personally; and the Bible was written to tell us how to attain to them.

We gain salvation by seeking God and letting Him work through us.

The Lord is my light and my salvation (Psalm 27:1).

He only is my rock and my salvation (Psalm 62:2).

He hath raised up a horn of salvation for us . . . (Luke 1:69).

And all flesh shall see the salvation of God (Luke 3:6).

Such texts as these are typical of the Bible promises concerning salvation.

Salvation comes to a few people gently and easily, but the majority have to work out their salvation with a certain amount of "fear and trembling" for the time being. The actual way in which it comes is not really important, for come it will—when we seek it with our whole heart.

WICKED

The word *wicked* occurs more than three hundred times in the Bible and is one of the most important terms to be found therein. In the Bible the word *wicked* really means "bewitched" or "under a spell." The Law of Being is perfect harmony, and that truth never changes, but man uses his free will to think wrongly, and thus he builds up false conditions around him, and then believes them to be real. They look real, and so he forgets that it was he himself who made them, and thus he bewitches himself, or throws himself under a kind of spell; and of course as long as he remains bewitched he has to suffer the consequences. Nevertheless, it is only illusion, or a spell, and it can be broken by turning to God.

The only way to break such a spell is to think of God. *O foolish Galatians, who hath bewitched you . . . ?* (Galatians 3:1), said Paul, when he heard that some of his students had begun to believe evil in this way. *The wicked flee when no man pursueth* (Proverbs 28:1).

Let us awaken from the spell under which the whole race lives, and know instead that God is all Power, infinite Intelligence, and boundless love.

Let the wicked forsake his way, and the unrighteous man his thoughts: and let him return unto the Lord, and he will have mercy upon him . . . (Isaiah 55:7).

JUDGMENT

Judgment, in the Bible, means deciding upon the truth or falsity of any thought. This process necessarily goes on in our minds all the time we are awake, and the extent to which we "judge righteous judgments" determines the character of our lives. To accept evil at its face value is to judge wrongly, and bring its natural punishment. To decline to believe in evil and to affirm the good is righteous judgment and brings the reward of happiness and harmony.

Thus *The Judgment* is not a great trial to take place at the end of time; it is a process that goes on every day. When Jesus said, *judge not, that ye be not judged* (Matthew 7:1), he meant that to condemn our brother out of hand instead of seeing the Christ within him, is to put ourselves in danger, because we are making a reality of those appearances in him, and whatever we make real we must demonstrate in our own lives.

REPENTANCE

To repent means, really, to change one's mind concerning something. When a person realizes that a particular action, or a certain line of conduct, or perhaps the whole direction of his life, has been wrong, and honestly resolves to change his conduct, he has repented. The Bible makes true repentance an essential condition for any spiritual progress, and for the forgiveness of sin. Jesus said, *Except ye repent, ye shall all likewise perish* (Luke 13:3).

Repentance does not mean grieving for past mistakes, because this is dwelling in the past, and our duty is to dwell in the present and make this moment right. Worrying over past mistakes is remorse, and remorse is a sin, for it is a refusal to accept God's forgiveness.

John the Baptist said, *Repent ye: for the kingdom of heaven is at hand* (Matthew 3:2). This means that you should change your thought and know that the Presence of God is where you are.

LIFE

Jesus said that he had come that we might have life and that we might "have it more abundantly." The Bible often uses the word *life*, and always with the implication that it is the greatest of all blessings. *With long life will I satisfy him* (Psalm 91:16). *Thou wilt show me the path of life . . .* (Psalm 16:11). *Keep thy heart with all diligence, for out of it are the issues of life* (Proverbs 4:23). Jesus says that those who follow him shall have the light of life. And the great goal of man is said all through the Bible to be eternal life.

Now what is this life of which the Bible speaks? You experience life when you feel yourself to be free and useful and joyous, and unconscious of either fear or doubt. Everyone has known such periods. Though they are much rarer than they should be, those are the times that you were alive. At other times you did not have life, in the Scriptural sense.

So when the Bible promises us long life, under certain conditions, it promises us a long period of joy and freedom. When it promises eternal life, it promises the enjoyment of these things forever, on the condition that we keep the Great Law—by seeking more knowledge of God, and putting Him first in our lives.

Healing is only the beginning. When you are completely healed of everything wrong in your life—your body, your business, difficulties in personal relationships, obvious faults in your own character—you will not have finished your work. Your real work will only be commencing.

Your real work is to show and experience the glory of God, to build the spiritual consciousness, "the house magnifical." Conscious fear will have gone, and your whole world will be different. The physical world will be different because it will be clothed in a new glory— "the light that never was on sea or land." Then people will be different because you will be beginning to know their real selves instead of merely the outer shell, and, of course, everyone else will notice that you are different, too.

This is not to say that healing is unimportant—it has to precede the building. Let us endeavor to get our own healing completed as soon as possible in order to help the world that is needing it so much.

Bless the Lord . . . who healeth all thy diseases . . . who crowneth thee with lovingkindness . . . (Psalm 103:2–4).

The body cannot resist healing. It cannot even try to resist it. It cannot, so to speak, even want to resist it, because it is not intelligent. It is important to understand this fact when praying for your own healing or that of another because otherwise, without realizing it, you are likely to enter on a mental struggle with the body to compel it to change; and, of course, such a proceeding is quite useless and also fatiguing. It is your sincere belief about your body that has to be changed—changed from false belief to the Truth.

Then . . . thine health shall spring forth speedily: and thy righteousness shall go before thee . . . (Isaiah 58:8).

I know when people pass by me in a line who it is that wants advice. They have to tell me their story in a minute; I have to get their story straight and they have to come to the point. As a rule they don't. They usually say instead, "I am not going to take up your time. I know a public man doesn't have much time. I thought if I could just talk to you and tell you what is in my mind . . ." But why don't they do it? Because they are worried so that they cannot say what is on their mind. If I may seem impatient, do forgive me. I know if you have a problem it will be difficult for you to come to a point. If you could, it would not be much of a problem. But this I can say to you: In my work I have every sort of person coming to me for advice and help. I have been doing this work now for many years, and there is not any kind of person who has not told me everything about himself. I have never found a case that couldn't be changed and put right if the patient would cooperate.

One generation shall praise thy works to another, and shall declare thy mighty acts (Psalm 145:4).

The only subject that matters is getting an understanding of Truth, developing our souls; but in order to develop our souls we must have some knowledge of the power of concentration. If you can learn and practice right concentration, there is no good thing in the universe that you cannot attain. Concentration means literally "bringing to a common center." Until you can put your attention where you want it you have not become master of yourself. You will never be happy until you can determine what you are going to think about for the next hour.

First, make your body comfortable, then tell it to be good until you come back for it. Concentration has nothing to do with the muscles, it has nothing to do with the blood vessels. Concentration means thought control. It is purely a mental thing and if you are rightly concentrating you will find that you are actually relaxed.

People imagine that concentration means holding on to one thought. The human mind is so constituted that it is impossible to do that. True concentration is a movement of the mind along a predetermined path. Nineteen people out of twenty people who say they have failed in concentration have been trying to stand still mentally. All people do have good powers of concentration, but not when they want them. You always concentrate on what you are interested in.

I can do all things through Christ which strengtheneth me (Philippians 4:13).

261

I do not give exercises to develop concentration. Concentrate on what you are doing at any time, that is the best exercise I know.

I remember when I was a boy about twelve years old somebody gave me a perfect peach of a jackknife. It probably weighed a quarter of a pound and there was a little saw in it, a little screwdriver, a corkscrew, a thing for getting stones out of horses' hoofs, and several blades. I carried it for about a year thinking how handy it would be for certain cases that never came up, but it never lost its interest. I could always find, when I was bored, new interest when I took out the jack-knife. If you make your search for God your jackknife in that sense, you will get your concentration and you will get your success.

Thus will I bless thee while I live . . . and meditate on thee in the night watches (Psalm 63:4, 6).

If you seem to yourself to be lacking in certain necessary qualities, seek that aspect of God which will meet your lack. If you seem to lack strength, ask God to give you what you need. Remember you can build any quality into your mentality by meditating upon that quality every day. You have created your limited self by thinking and you can destroy it at any moment by thinking a new pattern.

Why do we not change from day to day, and week to week, from glory to glory, until our friends can scarcely recognize us for the same man or woman? Why should we not march around the world looking like gods, and feeling it; healing instantaneously all who come to us; reforming the sinner; setting captives free?

The spirit of the Lord God is upon me; because the Lord hath anointed me to preach good tidings unto the meek; he hath sent me to bind up the broken-hearted, to proclaim liberty to the captives, and the opening of the prison to them that are bound (Isaiah 61:1).

The Bible is the most Precious possession of the human race. It shows us how to live. It meets everyone on his own level and brings him to God. Nevertheless, its real value lies in our interpretation of it.

Hear a Parable: A remote island was inhabited by highly intelligent savages. They had some primitive art and made excellent drawings of animals on the walls of caves. A box was washed ashore containing a number of books, dry and in good condition. The natives were delighted and pored over these pages admiring the odd shapes and patterns made by the letterpress—totally unaware of the real meanings behind it all; unaware of the very existence of Falstaff, or Portia, or Hamlet; of Huckleberry Finn, and of the other characters who lived in the books.

If you have been reading the Bible without the spiritual interpretation you are in just that position.

Ye do err, not knowing the scriptures (Matthew 22:29).

Are you double-minded? Jesus says that a double-minded man is unstable in all his ways, and that such a person need expect nothing from the Great Law.

If any of you lack wisdom, let him ask of God, that giveth to all men liberally, and upbraideth not; and it shall be given him. But let him ask in faith, nothing wavering. For he that wavereth is like a wave of the sea driven with the wind and tossed. For let not that man think that he shall receive any thing of the Lord (James 1:5–7).

This is very obvious common sense. If you affirm one thing now, and the opposite in half an hour; if you meditate helpfully and then go downstairs to talk trouble; it is entirely natural that you should fail to influence people with the peace that comes with prayer.

If you stepped into a taxi at Grand Central and told the driver to take you to Central Park, and then, after a block, told him to drive you to the Battery, and then after a couple of blocks asked him to go to Central Park again, you could hardly expect the driver to land you at any destination. And yet this is what a good many of us do in practice. We affirm both harmony and disharmony until the subconscious mind is completely muddled, and, of course, our lives are in confusion.

Where our words and deeds reinforce one another the effect is powerful and the result certain. Where they are not in accord they cancel out, leaving us where we started, or more likely worse off.

We do not make our spiritual unfoldment in a steady straight line. Human nature does not work in that way. No one moves upward in a path of unbroken progress to the attainment of perfection. What happens is that we move forward steadily for a while, and then we have a little setback. Then we move forward again, and presently we may have another setback. These setbacks are not important as long as the general movement of our lives is forward.

The tide flows in and out. The foremost wave comes in and in, and it seems as though it would never stop until it reached high-water mark—but it does stop, and actually goes back, and if one did not know better he would suppose that that was the end of the matter. But it is not. The tide goes back a little, but not to its old mark, and then it comes on again and this time it makes a higher mark. This mode of progression seems to be general throughout nature.

Do not watch the individual waves but keep your attention on the tide, and all will be well.

Then he said unto them, Go your way . . . for the joy of the Lord is your strength (Nehemiah 8:10).

Many people think they would like to be what is called dynamic but it does not appear that they always have a very clear idea of what that expression really means. Aggressive and noisy? Bombastic, in manner?

A dynamic person is one who really makes a difference in the world; who does something that changes things or people. The magnitude of the work done may not be great, but the world is different because that person has lived and worked. The real secret of a dynamic personality is to believe that God works through you, whatever you may be doing; to put His service first, and to be as sincere, practical, and efficient as you know how.

. . . know thou the God of thy father, and serve him with a perfect heart and with a willing mind . . . (1 Chronicles 28:9).

The present moment is never intolerable. It is always what is coming in five minutes or five days that makes people despair. The Law of Life is to live in the present, and this applies to both time and place. Keep your attention to the present moment, and in the place where your body is now. Do a fair day's work, and then stop. Overwork is not productive in the long run.

A friend of mine was visiting a great cathedral in Italy. Just inside the door was a magnificent mosaic extending the width of the building, but not yet completed. It represented the Last Judgment and the number of tiny pieces of different colored marble involved in it staggers the imagination. A man was on his knees working away and my friend, who spoke Italian, whispered to him, "What a stupendous task you have! I could not even dream of undertaking so much work."

The man replied quietly, "Oh, I know about how much I can do comfortably in one day. So each morning I mark out a certain area, and I don't bother my head thinking outside of that space. Before I know where I am the job will be complete."

Take therefore no thought for the morrow: for the morrow shall take thought for the things of itself . . . (Matthew 6:34).

In the old fairy tales we were often told that when a little prince was born the fairies came to the christening with gifts. One is tempted to ask what gifts we would choose for ourselves if we had the ordering of such matters. What are the three best gifts that a child could be born with?

I suggest the following three: a good constitution, a good disposition, and horse sense. I think that a child endowed with these three qualities would have very few difficulties to meet in life.

I put a good constitution first because health is the greatest of all human blessings. On the other hand, people do not always realize how much difference a good disposition makes in oiling the wheels of everyday life. Finally, plain sense. I believe that horse sense, as it is called, is more important than the possession of any kind of mere ability or even great talents. We have all known men and women of the utmost brilliance, who apparently had every gift for success in life, but who, owing to a lack of simple, plain sense, came to shipwreck.

Now, supposing you feel that you were not endowed with one or any of these gifts, what can you do? Well, the Jesus Christ teaching tells us that no good thing for which we pray is withheld. If you want any of the above gifts for yourself, pray for it each day, by claiming it; and build it into your character by acting the part in every circumstance that arises.

. . . *What things soever ye desire, when ye pray, believe that ye receive them, and ye shall have them* (Mark 11:24).

The one great enemy of the human race is fear. The less fear you have, the more health and harmony you will have. The only real problem of mankind is to get rid of fear. When you really do not fear a situation it cannot hurt you. Of course, you must remember that fear often exists in the subconscious mind without your necessarily being aware of it. The great thing to remember is that fear is a bluffer. Call its bluff, and it collapses.

An amusing incident happened in Holland a number of years ago. A lion escaped from a traveling circus. Not far away a good housewife was sewing near the open window of her living room. The animal suddenly sprang in, dashed by her like a flash, rushed into the hall, and took refuge in the triangular cupboard under the staircase. The startled woman supposed it to be a donkey and, indignant at the muddy prints it left on her clean floor, pursued it into the dark closet among the brooms and pans, and proceeded to thrash it unmercifully with a broom. The animal shook with terror and the angry woman redoubled the force of her blows. Then four men arrived with guns and nets and recaptured the animal. The terrified lion gave himself up quietly, only too glad to escape from that dreadful woman.

When the woman discovered that she had been beating a lion, she fainted away.

This story illustrates perfectly the demoralizing power of fear. Our good housewife completely dominated the lion as long as she thought he was a donkey, and as long as she treated him as a donkey the lion was in abject fear of her. When she discovered her mistake, the old race fear came back and she still reacted in accordance with the race tradition.

. . . *He that feareth is not made perfect in love* (1 John 4:18).

We are all engaged in building our consciousness during every waking hour. This work is invisible, silent, and consequently overlooked by the bulk of mankind. Nevertheless, it is the most fundamental and the most far-reaching activity in life. Hour by hour, and moment by moment, we are building good or evil, failure or success, happiness or suffering into our life by the ideas that we harbor, the beliefs that we accept, the scenes and events that we rehearse in the hidden studio of the mind. This fateful edifice, upon the construction of which we are perpetually engaged, is nothing less than our self—our personality, our identity on this earth, our very life story as a human being.

That wondrous building, the spiritual consciousness, is called in the Bible the Temple of Solomon, and we are told two wonderful things about that building. It was built without any noise (and we know that thought is soundless), and it was built upon a rock.

And the house, when it was in building, was built of stone made ready before it was brought thither; so that there was neither hammer nor axe nor any tool of iron heard in the house, while it was in building (1 Kings 6:7).

. . . be thou my strong rock, for a house of defense to save me (Psalm 31:2).

I once came across an old sermon that was delivered in London during the French Revolution. The author said, referring to the Sermon on the Mount: "Surely it is justifiable to hate the Arch-Butcher, Robespierre, and to execrate the Bristol murderer." This pronouncement perfectly illustrates the fallacy that we have been considering.

You might just as well swallow a dose of prussic acid in two gulps, and think to protect yourself by saying, "This one is for Robespierre; and this one for the Bristol murderer." You will hardly have any doubt as to who will receive the benefit of the poison.

A woman said: "I have a right to be angry," meaning that she had been the victim of very shabby treatment. This, of course, is absurd. There is no one to give such a permit, and if general laws could be set aside in special instances, we should have, not a universe, but a chaos. If you drank a deadly poison inadvertently, you would die because such is the law. For the same reason, to entertain negative emotions is to order trouble—quite independently of any seeming justification that you may suppose yourself to have.

Keep thy heart with all diligence, for out of it are the issues of life (Proverbs 4:23).

A man came to see me in London in great distress. He had attended some lectures I gave, and wanted advice. He was the owner of a general grocery store in a village in the south of England, and hitherto there had been no competition. Now, one of the big chain stores was opening a branch almost opposite to him in the main street, and he was in a panic.

He said, "How can I compete with them? I am ruined."

I said, "You know the Great Law. You know where your supply comes from. Why be afraid?"

He said, "I must do something."

I said, "Stand in your shop each morning and bless it, by claiming that divine Power works through it for great prosperity and peace for all concerned." He nodded his head in agreement.

I added, "Then look down the street to where they are fitting up the new store, and bless that in the same way."

"What? Cut my own throat?" he almost screamed.

I explained that what blesses one, blesses all. I told him that he was really hating his competitor (through fear) and that his hatred would destroy him, while blessing the "enemy" was the way to get rid of hate. I finished by saying, "You cannot cut your throat with prayer; you can only improve everything."

It took some time to persuade him, but at last he got the idea, and when I met him several years later he told me that his business had been better than ever since the chain store appeared; and that it seemed to be getting on well too.

This is what Jesus meant when he said, *Love your enemies* (Luke 6:27).

Read Psalm 18.

Everyone knows today that man's greatest enemy is fear. If you really get rid of fear concerning any danger it has no power to hurt you. It is no mere platitude to say, "There is nothing to fear but fear." If you are afraid about something, read this psalm—carefully and thoughtfully, realizing the spiritual meaning of each verse, and very soon your fear will begin to lessen, and will finally disappear.

The advantage of a written prayer like this is that it makes you think powerful thoughts, and, as you know, it is the right thought that demonstrates. The change brought about in your thinking does the work.

The psalm opens with an affirmation of faith in God. Always begin every prayer by affirming your faith and trust in God: *I will love thee, O Lord, my strength.*

Then you go on to say that God is your rock, and your fortress, and your deliverer, your strength and your buckler. You think of Him as the horn of your salvation and your high tower. The horn is a symbol of plenty, and, of course, a high tower is a safe place. If you hold to your faith in God it is only a question of time before you will be free and therefore safe.

Read Psalm 18:8–16.

Thinking of one of his own experiences, the Psalmist says that the sorrows of hell compassed him about and the snares of death came upon him, and that he "cried unto God"—he went on praying—and that God came to his rescue. He says that the earth shook and trembled and that the very hills moved because God was wroth. Of course, the "earth" means your environment, and all the outer conditions that constitute your life experience at the present time. Thus the shaking and moving of these things means that all your conditions are being changed, naturally for the better. The "wroth" of God in the Bible always means the activity of God. It does not mean anger.

. . . *and the Highest gave his voice* . . . (Psalm 18:13).

Read Psalm 18.

In verse 19 the Psalmist asserts, *he brought me forth also into a large place. . . .* Is it not a wonderful thought that God brings us forth into a large place? Then he adds that God delivered me, because he delighted in me. This verse really means that being delivered from the dungeon of fear, the Psalmist was beginning to experience the delight that peace of mind naturally brings.

And now comes a very significant statement, "according to the cleanness of my hands hath he recompensed me." This refers to right conduct or right living. To have clean hands means trying to live the Christ life. Our prayers have but little power if we are not honestly trying to live up to the best that we know. We always do what we believe.

With the merciful thou wilt show thyself merciful; with an upright man thou wilt show thyself upright; with the pure thou wilt show thyself pure; and with the froward thou wilt show thyself froward (Psalm 18:25–26).

This is a concise and powerful statement of the law that we literally reap what we sow. God, in His infinite wisdom, has made the Laws of the universe and left them to work themselves out. He is not constantly interfering in every individual transaction. If this were the case, there would be no law and God would not be Principle.

276

Read Psalm 18.

In verse 28 the Psalmist moves to another phase of the teaching. *Thou wilt light my candle: the Lord my God will enlighten my darkness.*

Many similes have been offered by religious teachers to illustrate the relationship between God and man. One of the best known and most helpful is to think of man as a spark from a great fire, which is God. The spark is not the whole of the fire but it is part of it, and therefore of the same nature, and possesses, potentially, all the characteristics of the parent fire. It can ignite many things upon which it falls, thus producing another fire essentially of the same nature as the original fire.

Read Psalm 18.

In verse 29 the Psalmist, thinking of some of the times in the past when he has been given power to overcome difficulties and to advance on the path, says, *For by thee I have run through a troop; and by my God have I leaped over a wall*. Everyone has found himself at some time confronted with a difficulty that seemed like a high and insurmountable wall, but faith in God enables one to clear the obstacle notwithstanding.

Next the Psalmist reminds us that the way of God is perfect. God will put you upon your high place. In other words, he will raise your consciousness so that you will automatically demonstrate. Then the author praises God and thanks Him for His goodness. Thanksgiving, as you know, is one of the most powerful forms of prayer.

Finally he says that God gives great deliverance to his king; and that He sheweth mercy to His anointed, to David and to his seed forevermore. God intends us all to be kings through the exercise of spiritual power, and our power to go on increasing—like the seed of David—through all eternity.

When the devil has been unmasked a number of times, his final refuge seems to be the harmless-looking word *but*. Students of the teaching of Jesus Christ who would not be deceived by any of the familiar devices, constantly surrender their principles, and therefore their demonstration, to the little word *but*.

"Of course I know that God is the only power—but—."

"Of course I know that God is omnipresent—but—."

"Of course I know that God is love—but—."

"Of course I know that there is no hurry because I am in eternity—but—."

"Of course I know that John or Mary must be the living expression of God, just as I am—but—."

If truth is true, there are no buts.

And they all with one consent began to make excuse (Luke 14:18).

Most people indulge in some form of daydreaming. There is no harm in this so long as such daydreams are positive and constructive in character. You are always thinking, when you are not asleep, and you know that it is in the selection of your thought that your destiny lies.

Do not let your daydreams take the form of an escape from actuality. A daydream is an evasion when it consists in fantasying something pleasant that nevertheless you believe could never happen. Such a daydream debilitates the whole mentality.

Some people daydream about all sorts of unpleasant things. They rehearse imaginary quarrels, imaginary injustices, accidents, and misfortunes, and because they do believe that such things could happen, and because thought is creative, they actually bring them upon themselves.

See to it that your daydreams are concerned with such happenings as you would really like to find in your life. Know that anything good is possible; remember the creative power of thought; and your daydreams will come true.

A double-minded man is unstable in all his ways (James 1:8).

Man has dominion over all things when he knows the Law of Being and obeys it. Do not put off your study of the law any longer. Take stock of your life this very day. Write down the things you *really* wish for. Be specific, not vague. Then write down underneath the conditions that you wish to remove from your life. If you do this candidly, you now have an extremely valuable analysis of your own mentality. In course of time this will tell you a great many things about yourself that you do not at present suspect, and as your knowledge of spiritual Truth increases, you will be able to handle the new knowledge about yourself in a surprising way.

Having gotten your main points in front of you, work on each one separately with all the spiritual knowledge you possess. Remember, it is not really very important how much of this knowledge you have so long as you make use of all that you do have. Repeat this treatment every day for a month, and by the end of that time it will be very unusual if a change for the better has not manifested itself in your conditions.

For those unfamiliar with spiritual treatment, an effective method of working is this: Claim gently but definitely that the great creative Life Force of the universe is bringing each of the needed changes into your life in its own way, in its own time, and in its own form. Do not try to dictate the exact form in which the new conditions shall come about. Do not be tense or vehement. Do not let anyone else know that you are doing this. Do not look impatiently every day for results.

Keep therefore the words of this covenant, and do them, that ye may prosper in all that ye do (Deuteronomy 29:9).

Who has not at some time or other planted a bulb and enjoyed the pleasure of waiting for the plant to appear and develop, and ultimately produce the glorious flower itself? Notice here that you naturally plant the bulb and expect the flower—the hyacinth or the crocus—to follow. No sane person would dream of planting the flower and expecting a bulb to come up; yet in our general life many of us do just that! We expect to begin with the flower. We think that we shall have desirable states of mind or body—happiness, freedom, health—if only we can change outer conditions in some way. Yet this is really trying to plant a flower, because we are trying to put effect before cause.

The law of the universe is thought first, and then expression; and never can this law be reversed.

Let all things be done decently and in order (1 Corinthians 14:40).

You cannot claim too much for yourself provided you claim the same thing for all other human beings. In fact, it is our duty to claim all good things and to continue claiming them until they demonstrate in our outer experience. Of course, this law works both ways and therefore you must be very careful not to claim the negative things that you do not want.

On the western ranches the owner of a steer brands it with his name, "Bar A Ranch" or some such cipher. Then if it should wander into strange territory, it will always be returned to him. On the other hand, when an animal without his brand wanders into his corral, he says, "That is not my steer," and out it goes.

Many a foolish person puts his mental brand on a steer that he does not want in the least, and is surprised when the animal stays obstinately at home. People say my rheumatism, my forgetfulness, my poverty, et cetera, branding the steers they do not want instead of turning them out of the corral.

When you really want something, brand it deeply with your own name and it will be yours.

. . . but every one . . . shall keep himself to his own inheritance (Numbers 36:9).

283

The capriciousness of destiny was a favorite subject with the old-fashioned novelists. In their three-volume world, people's lives were at the mercy of trifling accidents from day to day. A person's whole life was spoiled because one letter was stolen or went astray. The hero rose from obscurity to wealth and fame through meeting a casual stranger in a railroad car, or through saving someone from drowning at the seashore. One false step ruined an otherwise promising career.

All this is nonsense. We are not at the mercy of accidents for there are no accidents, and trifles have only trifling effects. In the long run your own character makes or breaks you. This is true of the individual, of a nation, of a party, or of any institution.

. . . *thou upholdest me in mine integrity* . . . (Psalm 41:12).

Don't pray or meditate as a duty. Realize that prayer is a visit with God and should be joyous.

Neither must you pursue your secular activities as necessary duties to be gotten over, that you may return to your prayer. In the light of Truth, there are no secular activities.

You must have regular recreation or you will become stale. Recreation, also, is to be enjoyed—as an expression of God—and not as a task to prepare yourself to pray better. An understanding joy in living is the highest prayer of all.

. . . *in thy presence is fullness of joy* . . . (Psalm 16:11).

W hen what seems an especially difficult problem or a great emergency presents itself, many students of Truth start by thinking, "This is very serious," and then proceed to brace themselves mentally for a supreme effort; and plan to pray exceedingly "hard" in order to meet the difficulty.

All this is quite wrong. It simply builds up the problem into something far bigger than it was originally. The right attitude, the one that brings Victory, is to think "God can and will solve this problem."

Instead of speaking the Word from the low altitude of fear and limitation, and trusting to effort to magnify the Lord, stop thinking of the problem altogether, and rise in consciousness. Having now attained a higher level—speak the Word gently from that level, and your problem will be solved.

For the word of God is quick, and powerful . . . (Hebrews 4:12).

A city child was spending his vacation on a farm. They showed him a hen sitting on a nest of eggs, and told him that some day a little chicken would come out of each egg. The child was delighted at this dramatic idea, and every morning he went around expecting to see the miracle.

Days passed, and nothing happened. The eggs still looked exactly the same. Not the slightest change occurred in the appearance of things, and gradually his faith waned. At last one day he told himself bitterly that he had been deceived.

Next day, however, from habit he went around to the nest as usual, but without any hope; and behold, what was his joy to see a flock of little chickens running about.

Of course wonderful changes had been taking place all the time, behind the shells, but there was nothing to show for it until the very last moment. Some of our greatest demonstrations come to us like this. In this story it was the spectator who lost faith, and so it did not matter. If the mother hen had lost her faith—well, there would have been no chickens. Give your demonstrations time to hatch.

And let us not be weary in well-doing: for in due season we shall reap, if we faint not (Galatians 6:9).

Is it selfish to pray for yourself? Some people think that it is, and say that you should pray only for others, but this, of course, is a foolish idea.

You must pray for yourself constantly. How could it be otherwise? We worship God by believing in Him, trusting Him, and loving Him wholeheartedly—and we can attain to that only through prayer. The sole object of our being here is that we may grow like him—and we can do that only through prayer.

The more we pray for ourselves the more power will our prayers have for any other purpose whatever; so praying for ourselves is the reverse of selfishness—it is truly glorifying God.

Bow down thine ear, O Lord, hear me: for I am poor and needy. . . . Rejoice the soul of thy servant; for unto thee, O Lord, do I lift up my soul (Psalm 86:1, 4).

The word *treatment* is usually applied to a prayer that is made for some specific purpose, as distinct from a general prayer, which is really a visit with God. You must remember that a treatment is a definite practical action, having a definite object and a definite beginning and end. It is in fact a surgical operation on the soul.

Let us suppose that you decide to heal a certain difficulty by prayer. You know that your difficulty must be caused by some negative thought charged with fear and located in the subconscious mind. You therefore turn to God, and remind yourself of His goodness, His limitless power, and His care for you. As you work the fear will begin to dissolve, and the awareness of the Truth corrects the erroneous beliefs themselves.

Thank God for the healing that you believe will come—and then you keep your thought off the matter until you feel led, after an interval, to treat again.

He sent his word, and healed them . . . (Psalm 107:20).

Seek ye first the kingdom of God, and his righteousness; and all these things shall be added unto you (Matthew 6:33).

The principle that Jesus expressed in these words is the basic law that underlies all answer to prayer. Many people know this in theory but are confused about putting it into practice. They think, "I will ignore this problem and think about God instead." Here there is a subtle mistake; because they are really thinking of their problem as existing in one place, of God as existing in another, and of themselves as going in thought from the first place to the second place. This, of course, is by implication to reaffirm the existence of the problem in its own place, and such a belief will not heal.

What we have to do is to seek the Kingdom in the very place where the trouble seems to be. We have to know that in Truth and reality it is not there, because God is there. When we succeed in doing this, the difficulty disappears.

Expect more from your prayers. The power of your prayer depends upon the amount of faith that you yourself have in it. To pray in the spirit that "even if this prayer does not do any good at least it cannot do any harm," is not, really, to pray at all.

Have enough faith in the love of God to believe that a short heartfelt prayer is just as good as a long one. Too long a session of prayer usually means that in your heart you really doubt the love of God, and think that a great deal of effort and toil will be necessary to move Him. Pray quietly and sincerely for a reasonable time—and then leave the matter, expecting success.

O Lord, thou art my God; I will exalt thee, I will praise thy name; for thou hast done wonderful things; thy counsels of old are faithfulness and truth (Isaiah 25:1).

Prayer is always the solution. No matter what kind of difficulty may be facing you, no matter how complicated your problem may seem—prayer can solve it. Of course you will also take whatever practical steps seem to be indicated, and if you do not know what steps to take, prayer will show you. Prayer is constantly bringing about the seemingly impossible, and there is no conceivable problem that has not at some time been solved by prayer.

When we remember that God really is omnipotent, untrammeled by what we call time or space or matter, or the vagaries of human nature, it is easy to see that there can be no limit to the power of prayer. You can pray about a problem and solve it at any stage, but of course the earlier you tackle it the easier will your work be.

. . . *The effectual fervent prayer of a righteous man availeth much* (James 5:16).

292

One is either on the Spiritual Basis or he is not, for there is no half-way house in this.

You are on the Spiritual Basis:

If you definitely give all power to God, in the most literal, practical, and matter-of-fact sense of the phrase.

If you really believe that prayer can do anything.

If you really believe that your happiness and well-being are vitally important in the eyes of God.

If you realize that whatever ideas and beliefs you accept must be expressed in your surroundings, and in all your relationships and activities.

If you try to see the Presence of God everywhere.

If, in short, you understand that you are in a mental universe, that things are thoughts, and that one's life history is fundamentally the expression of his belief about God.

Draw nigh to God, and he will draw nigh to you (James 4:8).

We all believe that the love of God is invincible. We all believe that His intelligence, His knowledge, and His power are infinite. We all believe that God cares for us to a degree beyond imagining, and that each one of us is equally precious in His sight. Yet, in many cases healing and harmony do not follow from this knowledge. Why is this?

In more cases it is because we have forgotten that these qualities have to be embodied in ourselves before they can appear in our lives. To know of them as existing in God is not sufficient. We must be seeking to express them in our personal lives before they can do anything for us.

The only way to know God is to seek to express Him in our lives.

It is a good thing to give thanks unto the Lord . . . to show forth thy lovingkindness in the morning, and thy faithfulness every night (Psalm 92:1–2).

Success consists in the overcoming of difficulties. All men and women who have made a success of any kind have done so by overcoming difficulties. There was a time when laying a telegraph line from New York to Boston presented many difficulties. Then there was a time when doing that was easy, but laying the Atlantic cable presented difficulties. Later on, marine cable laying became a routine business, but radio across the ocean presented problems that for a time were insuperable.

If you have a personal disability that seems to keep you from success, do not accept it as such, but capitalize on it and use it as the instrument for your success. H. G. Wells had to give up a dull underpaid job because of ill health, so he stayed at home and wrote successful books and became a world-known author instead. Edison was stone deaf and decided that this would enable him to concentrate better on his inventions. Theodore Roosevelt was a sickly child, very shortsighted and nervous. However, he worked hard to develop his body and became, as we know, a strong husky open-air man and big game hunter.

The owner of a fashionable dress business in London was the wife of a struggling clerk, who was stricken with tuberculosis. She had never been in business, and had no training, and found herself having to support a husband and two children. She started with nothing but good taste in clothes and a belief in prayer.

Problems are signposts on the road to God.

. . . To him that overcometh will I give to eat of the tree of life (Revelation 2:7).

Behind every problem or difficulty lies the Truth of Being. This means that in spite of the appearance, you must believe that divine Mind is already healing the situation. Jesus said that when you pray, believe that you have received. Often we are so close to a problem that, spiritually speaking, we accept the cloudy day as a permanent state of climate, forgetting that the sunshine of divine Love and Power has never ceased to shine, although obscured for the moment.

In prayer we remind ourselves again that, no matter how bleak or overcast the picture may be, we believe that in divine Mind there is nothing but good and therefore only good can express itself in these circumstances. The important thing is to raise your consciousness above the level where the difficulty seems to be, and put God there instead.

Then shall the righteous shine forth as the sun in the kingdom of their Father (Matthew 13:43).

In the gold rush days prospectors went out in the mountains in search of the yellow metal. Often the task was long and arduous with little to show for days of struggle and privation. But when a find was made, the prospector would stake his claim so that others would know that that particular discovery belonged to him. Of course, some claims turned out to be shallow veins of ore and worth little, while other claims eventually made their owners fabulously wealthy.

In metaphysics, we often speak of claiming our good, and it is one of the surest ways of bringing the good we desire into our lives. If we want health, then we have to claim every day that divine Life brings well-being to every part of our body. If we want prosperity, then we claim every day that God is the giver of every good gift, ready to supply our every need.

Whatever it is we wish to bring into our life, we *stake our claim to it.*

Of course, we often claim negative things for ourselves without fully realizing it. Every time we say, "My cold," "My headache," "My indigestion," we are claiming those things for ourself. What one claims for himself he will eventually bring into his life.

Affirm your divine kinship. All that the Father hath is ours—if we will stake our claim with God.

. . . *it is your Father's good pleasure to give you the kingdom* (Luke 12:32).

The Bible tells us that God can heal us, that He can deliver us from our destructions, that He lifts up the weak, that He leads and guides us. But just how much can God do? Well, God can do almost anything. That may sound strange to those who have been taught that with God all things are possible. But there are some things that God cannot do, and it is fortunate for us that this is true.

God is a God of love and rules by principle, and because this is so, He cannot change His nature. He cannot break divine law. He cannot bring disease, or suffering, or lack.

He is always the loving Father, ready to hear and answer prayer.

How much can God do? He can bring heaven here and now—not by breaking the law, which is impossible to God—but by fulfilling it.

Open thou mine eyes, that I may behold wondrous things out of thy law (Psalm 119:18).

When your knees are knocking together, and you do not know which way to turn—*think of God and His goodness*.

When prosperity seems out of the question—*give thanks for God's abundance*.

When you want peace of mind—*dwell upon the Presence of God*.

When your health is under par—*speak the healing Word*.

When you need inspiration—*browse through the Bible*.

When the situation seems to need a miracle—*remember that nothing is too difficult for God, and that He is performing miracles every day*.

I will not fail thee, nor forsake thee (Joshua 1:5).

Try this experiment today. Select one particular thing in your life that is not going well and you wish to make right. Next consider the matter in the light of your knowledge of God and of prayer. Realize that this thing cannot remain inharmonious or negative once you know the Truth about it. Realize that you are now knowing the Truth and claim that the divine Power in you is now healing the condition completely and permanently.

Then give thanks. Remember that praise and thanksgiving are the most powerful prayers of all.

The next day, repeat your thanksgiving, until the answer comes.

In between prayers you must keep your thought right concerning the problem. This is vital. All-day-long guiding of your thought cannot fail to bring your demonstration.

My meditation of him shall be sweet: I will be glad in the Lord (Psalm 104:34).

There is no use in merely saying everything will be all right. Thinking rightly, of course, means putting God into all your affairs and expecting him to change them. For example, if you are living in a shack it is not any good pretending that it is a palace. Cheap optimism is never spiritual. Realize that you are living in a shack, but claim the Presence of God to guide you to something better.

Teach me thy way, O Lord, and lead me in a plain path . . . (Psalm 27:11).

Years ago many devoted preachers and Sunday School teachers were fond of telling people to "pray hard." Well-meaning as this advice was, it was mistaken. I often tell people to pray "soft," which, of course, means gently.

I do this because I know that the more quietly and gently we pray, the better results we get. In prayer, as in many other activities, effort defeats itself. More than once I have said to my congregation, "Pray with a feather—not with a pickax."

Always pray gently, and especially if you have a good deal of fear, or if your difficulty seems to be a very important one.

For thou, Lord, art good, and ready to forgive; and plenteous in mercy unto all them that call upon thee (Psalm 86:5).

Man controls his own life. The Bible says that God has given him "dominion over all things," and this is true when he understands the Truth; and the Truth is that your outer conditions—your environment—are not cause; they are effect. You are not happy because you are well. You are well because you are happy. You do not have faith because things are going well. They are going well because you have faith. You are not depressed because trouble has come to you, but trouble has come because your realization of the Truth had first fallen off.

The secret of life then is to control your mental states. To accept sickness, trouble, and failure as unavoidable, and perhaps inevitable, is folly, because it is this very acceptance by you that keeps these evils in existence. Man is not limited by his environment. He creates his environment by his beliefs and feelings. To suppose otherwise is like thinking that the tail can wag the dog.

If you have been thinking that outer conditions are stronger than you are, say to yourself: "Tail wags dog" and immediately reverse the belief.

. . . *who did hinder you that ye should not obey the truth?* (Galatians 5:7).

Of what does the consecrated life consist?

Your life is a consecrated one when you are ready at all times to do the will of God—when you are willing and anxious that God may be fully expressed through you, through your thoughts, words, and deeds, during every hour of the day.

You are not concerned with the question of results. Results belong to God.

Here am I; send me (Isaiah 6:8).

W hen you have to make a decision or take a certain action, all that you can do is to do the best you know *at that time*, and if you do that you will have done your duty. In the light of after events it may turn out that you made a mistake, but that will not be your fault because you could not possibly do better than the best you know at the time.

Claim that the Christ is guiding you; and believe it, and the ultimate outcome will be favorable even if things seem to go wrong for a time.

And the Lord shall guide thee continually . . . (Isaiah 58:11).

Most people feel intuitively that the simplest things in life are the most important, or, if you prefer, that the most important things in life are found to be the simplest. This is a very profound discovery. What is more important to us than breathing, for instance?

Another simple thing that is of great moment is a smile. A smile affects your whole body from the skin right in to the skeleton, including all blood vessels, nerves, and muscles. It affects the functioning of every organ. It influences every gland. Even one smile often relaxes a number of muscles, and when the thing becomes a habit you can easily see how the effect will mount up. Last year's smiles are paying you dividends today.

The effect of a smile on other people is no less remarkable. It disarms suspicion, melts away fear and anger, and brings forth the best in the other person—which best he immediately proceeds to give to you.

A smile is to personal contacts what oil is to machinery, and no intelligent engineer ever neglects lubrication.

Rejoice evermore (1 Thessalonians 5:16).

Do not dissect things too much. By the time you have dissected a living thing you have killed it, and you no longer have the thing that you began with. Take a rose out of the bowl, pull its petals apart, count them, weigh them, measure them, and then, while you will have certain interesting information, you no longer have a rose.

There is a place for analysis, but it is apt to be quite fatal in prayer and meditation. Do not dissect the love of God, but feel it. Do not dissect divine intelligence, but realize it. Do not wonder how God can possibly solve this problem, but just watch Him do it in His own way—and He will if you will give Him a chance.

You know that God is Love. So go ahead on that, and do not get theoretical about it.

Do you remember the old verse that says:

> A centipede was happy quite,
> Until a frog in fun
> Said, "Pray, which leg comes after which?"
> This raised her mind to such a pitch,
> She lay distracted in the ditch,
> Considering how to run.

The righteous shall be glad in the Lord, and shall trust in him; and all the upright in heart shall glory (Psalm 64:10).

God knows everything, and at all times. The Bible sometimes speaks of God as having changed His mind or being disappointed. God is supposed to have tested Abraham's obedience in the matter of Isaac. God is supposed to have had His plans upset by the misconduct of Adam and Eve, by the general wickedness of humanity before the flood, and, in fact, He is frequently represented as being disappointed and even frustrated by the conduct of mankind. In orthodox theology, the devil was continually upsetting God's arrangements and bringing his plans to naught. Indeed, to listen to some preachers, one would have supposed that the devil was a good deal more powerful than God.

Of course, all this is nonsense. Such things could not be really true of God. It was Abraham's *idea of God* that led him to prepare to kill Isaac. It was the wickedness of mankind in the antediluvian world that brought on the flood as a natural consequence, just as the fears, hatreds, jealousies, and greed of mankind over many years have brought on war.

We make an idolatrous image of ourselves and call it God. Let us destroy this image today and worship the true God who is infinite and unchanging Good.

God is not a man, that he should lie; neither the son of man, that he should repent . . . (Numbers 23:19).

You all know the Great Law. One way of stating it is to say: Like produces like. What we sow in thought we reap in experience.

People know that these things are true, and yet in spite of this transcendent knowledge they constantly use the Great Law for their own destruction. They would not dream of pouring water in the gas tank of their car, or sand into their watch, or broken glass into their food; but they do something just as foolish every time they think, speak, or act negatively. One cannot help wondering what such people have inside their heads—brains or excelsior.

In future, when you catch yourself thinking negatively, say to yourself severely, *"Brains or excelsior?"* and immediately switch to what you know to be the Truth of Being.

Knowing that whatsoever good thing any man doeth, the same shall he receive of the Lord . . . (Ephesians 6:8).

About the middle of the last century, a traveler was journeying along through what was then a remote part of South Africa. One day while smoking his pipe outside the hut in a native village, he noticed a group of little naked children playing what was evidently a native version of the time honored game of marbles. He watched the game idly for a while, and then something about the rough stones caught his attention. They were quite small pebbles, dull, but—here his pulse began to steeplechase. He spoke to the children's father, with studied carelessness, and the Kaffir said, "Oh yes, the children like these little stones. They have some more in the hut," and he brought forth a small basket containing several more.

Repressing his excitement, the traveler took out a large plug of tobacco, worth perhaps twenty or thirty cents in our money, and said, "I would like to take the stones home for my children. I will give you this tobacco for them. Are you willing?" The Kaffir laughed and said, "I am robbing you but if you insist, all right," and the bargain was sealed—which not only enriched the stranger but led in time to the great discovery of the South African diamond fields.

The fate of the Kaffir is really the fate of most human beings. Man holds a fabulous treasure in his possession—the power of the Spoken Word—and yet, in most cases, he does not know it.

The Lord shall open unto thee his good treasure . . . to bless all the work of thine hand . . . (Deuteronomy 28:12).

True salesmanship means finding out what your customer really
needs, and supplying him with it; or if you cannot furnish it yourself,
advising him to go elsewhere. Such a policy will not mean loss of
business. On the contrary, working in this way you may lose one order
but you will get half a dozen in its place—and you will have peace of
mind. Any one particular sale does not matter; it is the annual
turnover that counts.

The policy, the Golden Rule, was taught by Jesus, the wisest and
most practical teacher who ever lived. Salesman treat your customer
exactly as you would like him to treat you if the positions were reversed. Tell him exactly what you would like to be told about the
merchandise, if you were the purchaser; and if you will do this the
whole universe will cooperate to make your business career an out-
standing success.

Teach me to do thy will, for thou art my God: thy spirit is good . . .
(Psalm 143:10).

Some wonderful demonstrations come at the eleventh hour. Others come at the twelfth hour. And some of the deepest and most far-reaching demonstrations come at the thirteenth hour—if you maintain the right attitude. What, after all, is the right attitude? It is simply knowing the Truth of Being instead of accepting the error.

Many people are aware of this, and they work in the right way—for a while. If, however, the demonstration has not arrived a little before the eleventh hour, they give up in despair, and naturally their prayer is not answered. But, this can only mean that they do not really believe.

If your statements of Truth are true, they are true whether the victory comes at eleven or twelve or one o'clock. State the Truth of Being concerning the problem. Hold to it even after twelve o'clock has struck, and you will be surprised at the wonderful good that can come to you at the thirteenth hour.

The Lord's hand is not shortened, that it cannot save, neither his ear heavy, that it cannot hear (Isaiah 59:1).

Have you heard the old story of the two *spirations?* They are essential for every worthwhile achievement. If either is missing the enterprise is doomed to failure, and if you have not been making your life as successful as you would like, you must go to work and find which of them has been overlooked. I am sure it is hardly necessary to tell you that the two spirations in question are *inspiration* and *perspiration*.

First you need *inspiration*. Sheer hard work, blind plodding, or brutal hammering will not bring success. You must also have regular *inspiration*.

Second, *perspiration*. There is no success without persevering hard work in the direction of your goal. Recently I heard one of the greatest living musicians address a class of musical students. He said, "I know of no road to success except hard work. If there is such a road I have not heard of it."

I added in my own thought, "Work hard—but do not make hard work of it."

Contact God daily for inspiration; and *then* work hard.

Except the Lord build the house, they labour in vain that build it; except the Lord keep the city, the watchman waketh but in vain (Psalm 127:1).

In the spiritual teaching we are told not to dwell upon our troubles, but instead, to realize the Presence of God where the troubles seem to be. Critics have suggested that this policy is "running away from life." Is it?

Suppose you found yourself in a house that was on fire; what would you do? You would leave the burning building as rapidly as possible. Would this be running away from life? Would it not rather be seeking life?

Sickness, sin, fear, and limitation—these things are not life—they are partial death; and they are to be overcome by turning toward life, which is divine harmony.

To turn away from evil and realize God instead is to liberate yourself, to help the world, and to glorify God.

Look unto me, and be ye saved, all the ends of the earth . . . (Isaiah 45:22).

Someone said that living life is like playing a violin solo in public and learning to play the instrument as we go along. This saying describes the experience very well, but no one should worry about that. We are in this world for exactly that purpose—to learn.

While we are learning we do not expect to produce a perfect work. On this plane we are all students, and what matters is that each year we shall find the quality of our workmanship definitely better. People are sometimes depressed because their lives do not present a simple, logical, harmonious unfoldment, because their histories seem to be full of inconsistencies, repetitions, dead ends. This, however, is only to be expected during the learning period.

Your life has not been rehearsed. It is an adventure, and a discovery, and a training, and it is the final goal that matters.

And let us not be weary in welldoing: for in due season we shall reap, if we faint not (Galatians 6:9).

Peopople often say, "I try to do so-and-so, but I fail." The explanation for their failure is contained within the words themselves. You should never "try"; you should "let"—let God. When you "try" to do things, you are working from the outside. When you let God do them through you, you are working from the inside and success must come.

If you will reread the creation chapter in the Bible you will notice that God creates by "letting." God said "let," at every act of creation, and it was done. Now God creates by means of you if you will let him, but you must let. Someone said, "Let go and let God," and this is a wonderful recipe for overcoming fear or getting out of a tight place. In any case, the rule for creation is always to let.

Is any thing too hard for the Lord? (Genesis 18:14).

It is your duty to God to run your life on intelligent lines. God gives us all as much intelligence as we can possibly need, but, unfortunately, in most cases we use very little of it.

Ask yourself today if you are really conducting your life intelligently. Are you eating and drinking intelligently? Do you select your reading intelligently? Do you spend your money intelligently? Do you consider intelligently the things that you hear, or do you just accept them uncritically? Do you exercise intelligence in carrying out your daily work? Do you seek to approach each new problem with intelligence instead of mere emotion?

Have you intelligent plans for the future? Do you know what you would really like to do or to be, and if not wouldn't it be only intelligent to go to work and find out and then draw up an intelligent plan for gaining your desire?

The world needs more intelligence. There is plenty of will, but because people will not use enough intelligence, mankind everywhere is in difficulties. Your intelligence is the light of God in your soul.

Let this mind be in you, which was also in Christ Jesus (Philippians 2:5).

When you make a cake, you know that whatever you put into your mixing bowl will appear in the cake itself, and, on the other hand, that unless a particular substance does go into the mixing bowl, it cannot appear in the finished article.

The thoughts and beliefs that fill our minds ultimately appear in the cake of experience, and to realize this is to save oneself a lot of trouble. No one puts kerosene in the mixing bowl because no one wants it in the cake, for everyone knows that, if it does enter the bowl, in the cake it will be.

. . . they that plow iniquity, and sow wickedness, reap the same (Job 4:8).

It would probably be safe to say that more than half of the evil in the world is due to well-meaning busybodies who just cannot refrain from interfering. Needless to say, such people never have harmony or success in their own lives, for it is an invariable rule that he who minds his neighbor's business, neglects his own.

To interfere mentally in any situation involves you in the consequences just as much as would a physical interference. Of course, where it is your duty to concern yourself in any matter, you must do so—constructively and spiritually—and then the consequences to you can only be good.

For every man shall bear his own burden (Galatians 6:5).

*H*e *that passeth by, and meddleth with strife belonging not to him, is like one that taketh a dog by the ears* (Proverbs 26:17).

If, when those around you are talking negatively about something or someone, you chip in with your contribution, you are taking a strange dog by the ears—so look out! If you get emotionally entangled in what is not your affair, through indignation, self-righteousness, hatred, or otherwise, you have seized the dog again—and he will bite. And even to think negatively concerning such matters in the secret chamber of your own heart, will bring you proportionate and natural punishment.

It is always right to think rightly about any person or situation, and if you do this many opportunities will come to you to help people practically, without any breach of law, and without coming near the dangerous dog.

God has no office hours. There is never a time when God is unavailable. Day or night, summer or winter, God is always present; always ready to heal, to comfort, to inspire. It is not possible that you could turn to God in prayer without receiving help.

The one thing required of you is that you shall turn to Him wholeheartedly, and that you shall expect Him to act. The greater the emergency, the easier will it be to demonstrate. The most powerful of all prayers is simply "Be still, and know that I am God."

For the eyes of the Lord run to and fro throughout the whole earth, to show himself strong in the behalf of them whose heart is perfect toward him (2 Chronicles 16:9).

Perhaps the second best prayer ever written is the Scotsman's prayer—"Lord, give us a good conceit of ourselves." You cannot have too much respect for yourself. You cannot have too much confidence in yourself. You cannot claim too much for yourself. But remember that you must realize these things as being the expression of God in you and not independent qualities of your own. You must also accept them as being true for every other human being.

Nothing but failure can come of self-depreciation. Of course, it is true that stupid people can get the malady called "swelled head"— and this always ends in a fall—but the realization of one's divine self-hood never gives swelled head. It gives wisdom, balance, poise, and steady progress. Think, talk, live your divine, glorious selfhood, and it will demonstrate itself in your life.

I have said, Ye are gods; and all of you are children of the most High (Psalm 82:6).

Nothing is really worth worrying about. Nothing is really worth getting angry or hurt or bitter about. Positively nothing is worth losing your peace of mind over.

These important truths follow logically upon the following fact: You are going to live forever—somewhere. This means that there is plenty of time to get things right again if they have gone wrong. No matter what mistake you may have made, enough prayer will overtake it and cancel it. If those you love seem to be acting foolishly, you can help them with prayer to be wiser, and, meanwhile, if they suffer, it means that kindly nature is teaching them a lesson that they need to learn.

But suppose something awful should happen? Well, what then? Suppose you lost everything and landed in the poorhouse. What then? Think what a wonderful demonstration you could make there, and you would probably learn several valuable lessons there, and, anyway, it would be quite interesting. Suppose the whole universe blew up. What then? When the dust settles, God will still be in business and you will be alive somewhere, ready to carry on.

Cast thy burden upon the Lord, and He shall sustain thee: He shall never suffer the righteous to be moved (Psalm 55:22).

Never look back. Always go right ahead. Even if you are quaking, go right ahead. Jesus said the man who puts his hand to the plow and then turns back, is not worthy of the Kingdom of Heaven. He also said: *Remember Lot's wife* (Luke 17:32).

No matter how unattractive or how dangerous the road ahead may be, it is better than the road back. The road ahead may be veiled from sight—but you must teach yourself to regard the unknown as friendly. Remember that God is always on the road ahead.

. . . *cause me to know the way wherein I should walk; for I lift up my soul unto thee* (Psalm 143:8).

When you go down to the seashore, you find what is practically an unlimited supply of sea water at your disposal. There are billions upon billions of gallons there, but the amount that you can carry away will depend upon the vessel with which you have provided yourself. If you take a ten-gallon can, you can get ten gallons, but if you take only a pint pot you can take away only a pint, and if you have nothing bigger than a thimble, you would not be able to take away more than a thimbleful.

So it is with divine abundance. The only limit is the limit of our capacity to receive.

Thou openest thine hand, and satisfiest the desire of every living thing (Psalm 145:16).

A young doctor and his wife were entertaining an elderly aunt. After-dinner coffee was served, whereupon the visitor said excitedly, "John, you know I cannot drink coffee! The nicotine in it keeps me awake all night."

The nephew said, "I assure you, my dear aunt, there is no nicotine in this coffee." The aunt replied, "There is always nicotine in coffee, and it keeps me awake the whole night." The host then said, "My dear aunt, I assure you upon my word of honor as a doctor, that there is no nicotine in this coffee."

The old lady, who had the highest regard both for her nephew's professional qualifications and for his personal integrity, was satisfied; and thereupon drank three large cups of coffee, enjoyed them immensely—and slept like a top all night.

Naturally, there can be no nicotine in coffee; the old lady meant caffeine. Of course, one does not approve of the deception employed—deception is never legitimate—but the story illustrates perfectly the power of good and bad suggestion. The old lady first made a law of limitation for herself, and then repealed it without any trouble. Why not start today and repeal some of the many such laws you are sure to have made for yourself.

If thou canst believe, all things are possible to him that believeth (Mark 9:23).

For unto every one that hath shall be given, and he shall have abundance: but from him that hath not shall be taken away even that which he hath (Matthew 25:29).

This great text has been a stumbling block to many. It looks like injustice. It sounds like cruelty. Yet Jesus said it, and we know that he was always right.

The explanation is logical when you have the key to life. Your experience is the expression (pressing out) of your state of mind or consciousness, at any time. When your consciousness is high, everything goes well. When your consciousness is low or limited, everything goes wrong.

When trouble comes the usual thing is to meet it with fear, anger, disappointment, self-pity, or brutal will power. This naturally lowers the consciousness a good deal more, and things get still worse. From him that hath not (much) harmony, shall be taken away even that which he hath.

Harmony and joy naturally raise your consciousness and your faith in God still higher, and so things improve further. Unto everyone that hath shall be given and he shall have abundance. This is a simple statement of natural law. Let us thank God that this wonderful law exists.

Look where you are going because you will inevitably go where you are looking. Where your attention is, there is your destiny. Attention is the key to life. Whatever you really give your attention to, you become. Whatever you really concentrate upon will come into your life. The Bible says, *For as he thinketh in his heart, so is he* (Proverbs 23:7). It does not say simply as a man thinketh, but as he thinketh in his heart, and this means thinking with interest or feeling.

This law is often illustrated most amusingly in practical life. The "horsy" man with his equine looks, is known to us all. Kipling speaks of a Newfoundland fisherman who appeared for all the world like a great codfish himself; and Dickens speaks of a pedantic old lawyer who looked just like an animated roll of parchment. Keep your eyes open for these amusing dramatizations, and be sure to take to heart the tremendous lesson that they teach.

Mental relaxation is just as important as right mental activity. Wise relaxation and wise activity are the balanced poles of all true action. Many people are constantly subjecting their minds to totally unnecessary wear and tear.

We speak colloquially of "taking the train" somewhere and actually many people who ride in trains do take the train mentally the whole journey. Many years ago I noticed that when a train arrives in the terminal after a long run, the locomotive men always seem to come off the train looking fresher than most of the passengers; although they have been working and the passengers have not. The explanation is that for the engineer and fireman it was only a routine day's work. They did not "take the train" mentally—they let the engine take it.

The eternal God is thy refuge, and underneath are the everlasting arms . . . (Deuteronomy 33:27).

What do you really believe? It is as a man thinketh in his heart that matters, says the Bible, and this means the heartfelt conviction as distinct from mere formal assent.

If you want to know what you really believe, simply watch what you do. We always do what we believe, although we frequently talk differently. If you feel that you are not making the most of your life, change your beliefs. Your present beliefs must be wrong if they are not producing harmony and satisfaction.

Start believing in health; start believing in prosperity; start believing in the Christ in those about you; start believing that your own divine Selfhood is rapidly unfolding. Act as though you believed these things and the results will surprise you.

For there stood by me this night the angel of God, whose I am, and whom I serve, Saying, Fear not, Paul. . . . Wherefore, sirs, be of good cheer: for I believe God, that it shall be even as was told me (Acts 27:23–25).

In a certain museum in New York there are a couple of dinosaur's eggs on view. This exhibit appeals to the imagination. Visitors say, "Those eggs were laid millions of years ago, and here they are today untouched!" These people are apt to overlook the fact that for the dinosaur in question they represent complete failure. After all the trouble of laying those eggs nothing ever came of them.

It is surprising how many otherwise intelligent men and women waste the best days of their lives laying dinosaur's eggs that never hatch out. Either through lack of energy, or lack of intelligent planning, or failure to make God a partner, or more often sheer muddle-headedness, they lay an excellent egg and then stroll away and forget it. Do not start a plan unless you really think it is worthwhile, and if you are convinced that it is worthwhile, do not rest until you have brought it to fruition.

And Jesus said unto him, No man, having put his hand to the plough, and looking back, is fit for the kingdom of God (Luke 9:62).

In mining country one comes across a valueless substance that is so like gold ore that inexperienced people cannot always tell the difference. This is called Fool's Gold, and many a young prospector has wasted much time and hard work before discovering that he has been deceived by the spurious article. Old timers used to say to the tenderfoot: "When you think you have found gold you probably have not; but when you do find it, you will know it for certain."

So it is with the prospectors on the mountain range that we call life. There are many kinds of fools' gold to be found, but when you meet the genuine article you will have no doubt in your mind. The true gold will give you a sense of peace and poise, a sense of freedom and power because you will no longer be in bondage to passing material things. It will set you free from much of the tyranny of time and space beliefs. The true gold is that sense of the Presence of God with us, to obtain which is the object of this life.

Every good gift and every perfect gift is from above, and cometh down from the Father of lights . . . (James 1:17).

To be sensitive is good, because sensitive people are aware of a thousand interesting or beautiful things where the obtruse person gets nothing. To do any creative work you have to be sensitive; because the creative worker is a "receiving set" for divine Mind.

A world-famous tenor, who was literally fretting himself to death over unimportant matters, broke down in my office, and said that God was cruel to make him so sensitive. I replied, "If you had the hide of a rhinoceros you might be a happier man, but you would not be at the Metropolitan."

In an electric circuit any given point is said to be positive to any point below it, and negative to any point above it. Current passes always from the positive to the negative, and never the other way. Now, if you are positive in this sense to everything but the action of God, no negative things can come back at you. On the other hand, you are receptive (or "negative" in the purely electrical sense of this ambiguous word) to all good—the direct inspiration of God, the prayers of other people, and all the beautiful and interesting vibrations in the universe.

Here is an affirmation that, intelligently used, will save you much unnecessary bombardment by negative thoughts: I am positive to everything but the action of God.

For it is God which worketh in you both to will and to do of his good pleasure (Philippians 2:13).

333

Many years ago a professor wrote a book in which he said that he could always tell if a person were a potential criminal by the shape of his ear! This naturally created something of a furor, and a London newspaper sent a reporter to interview old General Booth, of the Salvation Army, on the subject. The reporter said, "General, you probably have an unmatched experience of human nature in the raw. Do you believe there is such a thing as a criminal ear?"

William Booth laughed loudly through his Mosaic beard, and replied, "Why, of course there is a 'criminal ear'—and we've all got one. If it were not for the grace of God, every one of us would be doing time or deserving to."

William Booth understood human nature. You never can afford to condemn another, because in his shoes you would probably have done just as badly. Have you not noticed that sometimes after condemning someone else rather pharisaically, you have shortly afterward caught yourself in a moral failure?

Wisely did the Master say, "Judge not."

But why dost thou judge thy brother? or why dost thou set at naught thy brother? for we shall all stand before the judgment seat of Christ (Romans 14:10).

The practice of tithing has been a lifelong habit with many. They think of their own money as amounting to 90 percent of whatever their net income happens to be and they set aside the 10 percent that belongs to God. The unfailing result is that such people are always free from financial difficulties. Though they may have other problems, they never remain in want.

Bring ye all the tithes into the storehouse, that there may be meat in thine house, and prove me now herewith, saith the Lord of hosts, if I will not open you the windows of heaven, and pour you out a blessing, that there shall not be room enough to receive it (Malachi 3:10).

And all the tithe of the land, whether of the seed of the land, or of the fruit of the tree, is the Lord's: it is holy unto the Lord (Leviticus 27:30).

Honour the Lord with thy substance, and with the first-fruits of thine increase: So shall thy barns be filled with plenty, and thy presses shall burst out with new wine (Proverbs 3:9, 10).

Jacob, after he had received the vision which told him that there is a mystical ladder reaching from earth to heaven—the ladder of scientific prayer and righteous activity—decided there and then to adopt the practice of tithing, realizing that God *will be with me, and will keep me in this way that I go, and will give me bread to eat, and raiment to put on, so that I come again to my father's house in peace* . . . (Genesis 28:20–21).

There is not the least obligation upon anyone to tithe until he reaches the state of consciousness when he will prefer to do so. To give grudgingly or from a supposed sense of duty, is really to give from a sense of fear. Some think that because they are in pressing difficulties it is impossible for them to tithe at the present time but they propose to do so as soon as circumstances improve. This is to miss the whole point—the greater the present necessity, the greater the need for tithing.

Give, and it shall be given unto you; good measure, pressed down, and shaken together, and running over, shall men give into your bosom. For with the same measure that ye mete withal it shall be measured to you again (Luke 6:38).

The secret of demonstrating prosperity in the spiritual way—and on no other basis can your prosperity ever be secure—is to know to the point of realization, that the one and only source of your supply is God, and that your business or employment, your investments, your clients or customers are but the particular channel through which that supply is at the moment coming to you from God. The practice of tithing is really the concrete proof that you have accepted this position.

Read Psalm 27.

The Twenty-seventh Psalm is one of the great meditations in the Bible. When trouble of any kind comes into our life it is because we have allowed our consciousness to fall to the level where fear and limitation can reach us. Any mental activity that enables us to raise the spiritual standard of the soul is a form of prayer, and the Bible abounds in such forms.

The history of solving a problem is often this: An individual is worried about something, or he feels ill. As soon as he realizes his state, he declines to accept the condition and proceeds to bring about the necessary raising of his thought. He reads this psalm carefully, interprets it spiritually, allows his mind to dwell upon the principles enunciated, appropriates them to himself, thus regaining his peace of mind.

The Lord is my light and my salvation; whom shall I fear? the Lord is the strength of my life; of whom shall I be afraid?

This one verse is one of the most complete texts in the whole Bible. It might well be written over the portals of every church and school in the land, for within it is contained in embryo the complete Jesus Christ message. It postulates not merely the existence of God but the living Presence of God in man. The Inner Light is no mere passive or static presence, but a dynamic power—light, salvation, and strength.

"The Lord is the strength of my life." Having promised us light, the psalm now goes on to promise strength or power. We are, in fact, to be "endued with power from on high" and need no longer trust to our own inadequate efforts.

This wonderful verse then sums up its great message in the word "salvation," and with the penetrating psychological skill, it obliges us to ask ourselves, point blank, what there is now to be afraid of.

Read Psalm 27.

When the wicked, even mine enemies and my foes, came upon me to eat up my flesh, they stumbled and fell.

"The wicked" and "mine enemies" stand for our own thoughts, for our fears and doubts of every kind; and truly indeed do they sometimes come upon us as though "to eat up our flesh."

Though an host should encamp against me, my heart shall not fear: though war should rise against me, in this will I be confident.

The Psalmist reiterates his confidence and makes us, his readers, reiterate that our hearts, too, shall not fear. When you can say quietly and truthfully at any hour of the day or night "my heart shall not fear," the world has no more power over you. You are free. War of various kinds may rise up against you, but you will be confident, and therefore you will be victorious.

One thing have I desired of the Lord, that will I seek after; that I may dwell in the house of the Lord all the days of my life, to behold the beauty of the Lord, and to inquire in his temple.

For in the time of trouble he shall hide me in his pavilion: in the secret of his tabernacle shall he hide me; he shall set me up upon a rock.

These two verses constitute a remarkable expression of what is often called the second birth. When you have reached that stage you do not allow any external happening really to grieve you, or frighten you, or hurt you, because you know that external things are but passing shadows of no permanent importance. This steadfast determination to dwell in the house of the Lord, to behold His beauty and to learn His secrets, means that you are set upon a rock and there your house of life is secure.

Read Psalm 27.

And now shall mine head be lifted up above mine enemies round about me; therefore will I offer in his tabernacle sacrifices of joy; I will sing, yea, I will sing praises unto the Lord.

This verse closes the first section with a burst of praise and thanksgiving and then moves into a form of supplication that is really affirmative. Praise and affirmation should be allied.

Hear, O Lord, when I cry with my voice: have mercy also upon me, and answer me.

When thou saidst, Seek ye my face; my heart said unto thee, Thy face, Lord, will I seek.

Hide not thy face far from me; put not thy servant away in anger: thou hast been my help; leave me not, neither forsake me, O God of my salvation.

When my father and my mother forsake me, then the Lord will take me up.

Teach me thy way, O Lord, and lead me in a plain path, because of mine enemies.

Deliver me not over unto the will of mine enemies: for false witnesses are risen up against me, and such as breathe out cruelty.

The Psalmist now prays for spiritual understanding and for peace of mind. The enemies, as always, are his own fears, and these fears take their rise in the fact that "false witnesses" rise up and confront him. And no one who has been through this experience will doubt the appropriateness of that telling phrase that our fears are things "such as breathe out cruelty." Verily, doubt and fear are the cruelest things that can come into the life of man.

Read Psalm 27.

I had fainted, unless I had believed to see the goodness of the Lord in the land of the living.

Here, the Psalmist once more makes it clear to his own mind that his reliance is indeed entirely upon the divine Power, and not upon his own limited intellect, or will power.

Wait on the Lord: be of good courage, and he shall strengthen thine heart: wait, I say, on the Lord (Psalm 27:13–14).

The closing phrase is a powerful exhortation to be active and steadfast in prayer. To "wait upon the Lord" does not in the least mean neglecting a problem in the hope that God will come along and solve it for you. Waiting on the Lord means praying constantly and systematically about your problem. No particular form of prayer is essential, but prayer there must be; that is, the conscious dwelling upon the Being of God.

If your intuitive nature is well developed, you will seldom need to use formal statements. This is excellent—for who will trouble to climb a ladder when he is strong enough to leap over the wall? However, many people lose the ability to receive intuitional messages when worried or frightened. Then the ladder will probably be their salvation.

Nevertheless, it must not be overlooked that very many people do all their praying with formal statements of Truth, but not through repeating affirmations like a parrot. Those who work like a parrot inevitably make the parrot's demonstration—they remain in the cage. Of a good prayer who used the same phrases many times it was said by a friend: "He constantly uses the old affirmations, but he stuffs them with fresh feeling every time."

Thoughtless people sometimes say that our affirmations and meditations are foolish because we state what is not so. "To claim that my body is well or being healed when it is not, is only to tell a lie," said one distinguished man some years ago.

This is to misunderstand the whole principle. We affirm the harmony that we seek in order to provide the subconscious with a blueprint of the work to be done. When you decide to build a house your architect prepares drawings of a complete house. Actually, of course, there is no such house on the lot today, but you would not think of saying that the architect was drawing a lie. He is drawing what is to be, in order that it may be. So, we build in thought the conditions that will later come into manifestation on the physical plane.

What is your intelligence for if not to be used in building the kind of life that you want? Very primitive men in prehistoric times rejoiced when they found food growing anywhere, and then they waited, perhaps for years, until they happened to find another crop. Today we use our intelligence, and plant in good time the actual crops that we want; and the amount that we consider necessary. We do not sit about hoping that wheat or barley may fortunately come up somewhere. If we did that, civilization would collapse.

The time has come when intelligent men and women must understand the laws of Mind, and plant consciously the crops that they desire; and just as carefully pull up the weeds that they do not want.

Then I told them of the hand of my God which was good upon me; . . . and they said, Let us rise up and build. So they strengthened their hands for this good work (Nehemiah 2:18).

Don't Hurry. You are going to live forever—somewhere. In fact, you are in eternity now; so why rush?

Don't Worry. You belong to God, and God is Love; so why fret?

Don't Condemn. As you cannot get under the other fellow's skin, you cannot possibly know what difficulties he has had to meet—how much temptation, or misunderstanding, or stupidity. You are not perfect yourself and might be much worse in his shoes.

Don't Resent. If wrong has been done, the Great Law will surely take care of it. Rise up in consciousness and set both yourself and the delinquent free. Forgiveness is the strongest medicine.

. . . *For there is no power but of God* (Romans 13:1).

Read Psalm 24.

The Twenty-fourth Psalm is the great summing up of the Bible teaching on letting God come into your life.

The earth is the Lord's, and the fullness thereof . . .

The key to the true meaning of this first stanza is found in the two pivotal words *Lord* and *earth*. In the Bible the word *Lord* means the I AM. The *earth* is a general term covering all expression or manifestation under the jurisdiction of the I AM. Now all trouble of every land really arises from the belief that the earth is subject to the dominion of some outer power or law that is able to govern it independently of the I AM. But the Law of Being is, that man is the image and likeness of God, and has full dominion over all his conditions, and this psalm emphasizes this wonderful fact by adding the world, and they that dwell therein.

Who shall ascend into the hill of the Lord?

The hill of the Lord, or His holy place, means the realization of God. It is that vivid, real sense of the Presence. When one attains to this he has a marvelous power of helping and healing others. To reach this state is the real object of all our prayers.

He that hath clean hands, and a pure heart . . .

But who are the pure in heart? Fundamentally, purity means complete loyalty to the belief in one single, all-embracing, Omnipotent God, Our Father which art in heaven. Hold unswervingly to God—this is purity.

To keep one's mentality consciously loyal to the One Power is only half the battle. The other half is to purify and re-educate the soul, not merely from the grosser sins that everybody recognizes, but from the thousand-and-one concessions to limitation belief that fill the everyday life of humanity. This is to have "clean hands," and to be able to ascend that wondrous "hill of the Lord."

Read Psalm 24.

He shall receive the blessing from the Lord, and righteousness from the God of his salvation.

This is the generation of them that seek him, that seek thy face. . . .

To many it may seem that the purification of the heart will be a long and wearisome task, but we have to remember that when we pray it is God who works and not we. If you will use the power of the Word, old habits of thinking will fall away and new ones come in; and this is because you will receive your righteousness, or right thinking, from God. You have sought His face, and you must begin to express something of His nature, for we always grow unto that which we contemplate.

Lift up your heads, O ye gates; and be ye lift up, ye everlasting doors; and the King of glory shall come in.

Gates and doors symbolize understanding and it is only by the attainment of a higher degree of understanding that the King of glory—the vivid realization of God which we are seeking—can come to our souls. We are then told to ask ourselves who the King of glory is, and for what He stands. He is nothing less than the Lord; strong and mighty in battle, and the battle he fights, of course, is our battle.

The Lord of hosts, he is the King of Glory.

People sometimes accept the idea that a change of thought, plus turning to God in prayer, will transform their lives into harmony and freedom. The logic of this principle appeals to them, and they set to work upon it in earnest. Then, after a few days, they say, "Nothing has happened after all," and they drop back into their old negative thinking.

That is extremely foolish. The results of many years of general negative thinking are seldom corrected in a few days. No one who goes upon a new physical diet or medical regimen expects to reap the advantages in so short a time. You must keep up the new way of thinking and refuse to be discouraged by seeming failures at first.

The right motive for adopting right thinking is that it is right, and that wrong thinking is wrong; and we should do right whether it seems to pay dividends or not. Of course, it does pay dividends—fabulous dividends—but it usually takes a little perseverance in the face of preliminary slowness.

And ye shall seek me, and find me, when ye shall search for me with all your heart (Jeremiah 29:13).

The Bible mentions the existence of an unforgivable sin, and this has greatly frightened innumerable Christians.

Let us be absolutely clear upon one point. There is no sin that a human being can commit that God will not forgive but there is one sin that he cannot forgive until we make it possible. This sin consists in shutting ourselves off from fresh inspiration or guidance from God. If your mind is already made up about everything appertaining to God; if you decide that you now know all the truth, and that you could not be mistaken; then it will not be possible for the Holy Ghost to open your eyes to error and lead you into higher truth. Naturally, as long as this is your state of mind, no help or improvement can come to you; and in that sense only is your sin unforgivable—unforgivable while it lasts. When you do change your attitude, enlightenment will come, and the sin will be destroyed.

Behold, I stand at the door, and knock: if any man hear my voice, and open the door, I will come in to him, and will sup with him and he with me (Revelation 3:20).

The only part of our religion that is real is the part we express in our daily lives. Ideals that we do not act out in practice are mere abstract theories. Actually, such pretended ideals are a serious detriment, because they drug the soul.

If you want to receive any benefit from your religion you must practice it; and the place to practice it is right here, where you are; and the time to do it is now.

A writer on prayer has said: "Knead love into the bread you bake; wrap strength and courage in the parcel you tie for the woman with the weary face; hand trust and candor with your coin you pay to the man with the suspicious eyes." This sums up the Practice of the Presence of God.

Give to him that asketh thee . . . (Matthew 5:42).

Why has not your prayer been answered? Perhaps it has. Strangely enough, it often happens that we receive an answer to our prayer and do not recognize it. Some of us have had demonstrations in our possession for weeks or months and have not known it. This mistake is caused by outlining. We have unconsciously decided that the demonstration must take a particular form, and because that form does not appear, we think we have failed. Actually we probably have an even better demonstration than we expected, but for the moment we are blind to it.

If a boy prayed for a man's hat (because he thought it would look well on him or make him grown up) he would not get it; since divine Wisdom knows that he could not wear it. He would get a good hat of the sort that would be useful to him. We often pray for things for which we are not really prepared; but if we pray scientifically this will not matter, since Creative Intelligence will send us the thing that we really need.

Seek God for His own sake, for the joy of being with Him, and demonstrations will take care of themselves.

I will be glad in the Lord (Psalm 104:34).

You cannot have your cake, and eat it too.

You cannot have peace of mind, and have your ailment too.

You cannot have a sense of divine Love, and have your jittery nervousness too.

You cannot have a feeling of toleration and kindliness and faith, and have your digestive troubles too.

You cannot have harmony continually unfolding in your life, and enjoy gossip and criticism too.

You cannot have power in prayer, and the luxury of resentment and condemnation too.

You cannot build a new consciousness and a new body, and live mentally in the dead past too.

. . . choose you this day whom ye will serve . . . but as for me and my house, we will serve the Lord (Joshua 24:15).

Buy the truth, and sell it not; also wisdom and instruction, and understanding (Proverbs 23:23).

All you have of Truth is what you understand of it—and what you understand you always demonstrate. It naturally follows from this that the only way to improve yourself and your conditions is to gain an increase in understanding. And the only way to gain an increase in understanding is to make practical use of the Truth you already know. Knowledge that you do not actually use is only intellectual knowledge and is barren, and even that fades out in time through lack of use.

You will never demonstrate or progress on mere theories that you have not put to the test. You will never demonstrate or grow spiritually on what is in a textbook or a lecture until you have begun to put such knowledge into practice. It is far better to have a thimbleful of spiritual knowledge and use it than to have a whole mountain of correct spiritual doctrine most of which you have never made work.

Think of God. Review some of the things that you know to be true about Him—His perfect goodness, infinite intelligence, all presence, limitless power, unbound love, and so forth. Claim that God who is all those things, is with you—and believe it.

Read a few verses of Scripture or any spiritual book that helps you.

Say silently that you forgive everyone who may seem to need it; without exception or mental reservation—and mean it.

Ask God to forgive you for all mistakes you have ever made; and say you accept His forgiveness—and mean it.

Claim that God is now inspiring you, teaching you, and healing you. Claim that He is giving you the greatest of all gifts—HIMSELF—because, having Him, you will have everything else too.

Give thanks in advance for the peace of mind, the harmony, and the spiritual growth that is yours—and mean it.

Offer unto God thanksgiving; and pay thy vows unto the most High (Psalm 50:14).

It happens to some students of prayer who are especially zealous, giving much time to study and meditation, and making more than average progress, that a time comes when their ordinary daily work begins to seem dull, tiresome, and really not worthwhile. Such a person may actually have a very important and interesting position, which most people would consider ideal; but now he is no longer content or happy. He would like to throw up business life altogether and devote all his time to his spiritual development.

The healing of this problem is first to know that a great many people have to meet it. It is not at all uncommon or peculiar to one person; and those who have it always come through it and find themselves happier than ever before because this particular difficulty only happens to wholehearted and zealous people. Such people usually spend too much time in prayer and meditation, and become waterlogged.

Having come through that stage they always find themselves more interested in their business than ever before; they do much better work, and at the same time they progress much faster in their spiritual lives, and have a great deal more power in prayer than they ever had before.

I know that thou canst do every thing, and that no thought can be withholden from thee (Job 42:2).

352

When you have driven the devil out of every other corner of your heart, his last refuge is to take shelter in negative analysis. He will say, "You prayed before and nothing happened," or, "You have been praying so long for that . . . " Or perhaps he will say, "There is no way that it can come about."

When this kind of thing comes into your thought, do not be discouraged but rather rejoice, for this means that satan is positively in his very last ditch, and now is the time to clear him out; and if you will be loyal to God it will not be difficult. Now is the time to know the Truth quietly, and to hold to it in spite of false appearances. Now is the time to witness to the faith that is in you. No finer opportunity for a great step forward spiritually can ever come to you than this one. So take advantage of it and rejoice in your good fortune.

It is not when things are going well that we make our progress. It is not even when things are going wrong and yet we feel sure that we can handle them with prayer, that we advance. It is when, smitten by the temptation to discouragement or even despair, we yet stand for what we know is the Truth, and say with Job, *Though he slay me, yet will I trust in him* (Job 13:15).

You form certain beliefs, for one reason or another—and then you have to live with them. When you were growing up, well-meaning people told you many negative things by way of warning, thereby implanting fears; and these fears are with you today, consciously or subconsciously. Other problems you brought here with you when you were born.

You meet your fears dramatized. The things that we fear in our hearts have a way of coming to us in the guise of other people's acts; of business conditions; of a breakdown in some part of the body.

Thank God it is not necessary as a rule to delve into the recesses of the subconscious and dredge for these things. In the spiritual teaching, as given in the Bible, we learn that by beating the symptoms spiritually (not, of course, covering up symptoms, but beating them) the fear or false suggestion that caused the symptom disappears too, and the patient is free.

Acquaint now thyself with him, and be at peace . . . (Job 22:21).

The principal reason why prayers are not answered is because in our hearts we limit the power of God. The Bible constantly tells us that the people got into trouble because they limited the Holy One. When you say, "There is no way out of my difficulty," what can it possibly mean except that you cannot see a way out? When you say, "It is too late now," what can that possibly mean except that it is too late for you?

When you pray you are turning to the power of God and surely you will admit that God is omnipotent, and therefore nothing can be too difficult, or too late, or too soon for Him. You will surely admit that Infinite Wisdom knows at least more than you do, to put the thing rather mildly. Well, Infinite Wisdom takes action when we pray and so our own limitations do not matter—unless we think they do.

Children often find themselves completely overcome by a difficulty that a grown-up person easily solves. What to the child seems an impossibility is quite easy to his father, and so even our greatest difficulties are simple to God.

Infinite Wisdom knows a beautiful and joyous solution to any dilemma. Do not limit the power of God for good in your life.

. . . *Is my hand shortened at all, that it cannot redeem? or have I no power to deliver?* . . . (Isaiah 50:2).

The world will take you at your own valuation. Your body will take you at your own valuation. Your business will take you at your own valuation; for the value that you really put upon yourself is the one that manifests. You may say, "But that cannot be true, because I know several people who are always boasting and pretending and yet no one ever takes them seriously."

Please note that I said the value you really put upon yourself. People who boast, bluff, and pretend have really a poor opinion of themselves—or why would they pretend? And it is this poor opinion or sense of inferiority that is demonstrated in the failure that such people always make of their lives.

The man who really believes that his wares are excellent does not dream of lying about them. The man who is satisfied with what he is has no incentive to pretend to be something he is not. The man who is conscious of substantial achievement has no desire to boast.

Nature always takes you at your own valuation. Believe that you are the child of God. Believe that you express Life, Truth, Love. Believe that Wisdom guides you. Believe that you are a special enterprise on the part of God—and what you really believe, that you will demonstrate.

Beloved, now are we the sons of God, and it doth not yet appear what we shall be . . . (1 John 3:2).

There is a quaint old legend that is firmly believed in the artists' colony in Paris. It appears that many years ago a poor struggling artist was so hard up that he did not have even enough money to buy a piece of canvas upon which to paint what he felt sure would be a masterpiece. Going along the quays he saw an old daub selling for a few sous, frame included. It was supposed to represent Napoleon III in full dress uniform, and doubtless had adorned some wall in the days of the Second Empire. That artist decided that he could clean off the picture and use the canvas for his own work.

Arrived home, he proceeded to remove Napoleon III, not a difficult task, and to his astonishment found that there was another picture underneath. The last artist had not even removed the original but simply worked over it. When the last traces of Napoleon III had disappeared, the student was amazed to discover what looked to him like a very fine Corot. He promptly submitted his find to the experts and it was pronounced a genuine Corot. Of course, his days of poverty were ended.

Whether this story be truth or fable, it is a perfect allegory of the nature of man as we know him. Outside we find the "marred image" showing limitation, sin, sickness, and inharmony—the unskilled daub; but underneath is the masterwork of the Great Artist, and our prayers act by clearing away the false accretions—the "many inventions" of the carnal mind—that the already existing Truth and harmony may appear.

Lo, this only have I found, that God hath made man upright; but they have sought out many inventions (Ecclesiastes 7:29).

Read Psalm 46.

Among all the beautiful and heart-searching prayers of the Bible there is none that surpasses the wonderful poem that we call the Forty-sixth Psalm.

It begins, as do nearly all the Bible prayers, with an expression of faith in God. This is extremely important in practice. You need to affirm constantly that you do believe in God, not merely as a vague abstract concept, but as a real, vivid, actual power in life, always available to be contacted in thought; never-changing and never-failing. The Psalm closes with a command and an affirmation.

Be still, and know that I am God. I will be exalted among the heathen, I will be exalted in the earth. This is really the whole Bible in a nutshell. *Be still, and know that I am God.* This is the very last thing that we want to do when we are worried or anxious. The current of human thought is always hurrying us along to its own ends, and it seems much easier to swim with it by accepting difficulties, than to draw resolutely away from these things, and contemplate God, which is the one way out of trouble. Even in your prayers there is a time to cease active work and, "having done all, to stand"—to *be still, and know that I am God.*

Life is a reflex of mental states. As far as you are concerned, the character that things will bear will be the character that you first impress upon them. Bless a thing and it will bless you. Curse it and it will curse you. If you put your condemnation upon anything in life, it will hit back at you and hurt you. If you bless any situation, it has no power to hurt you, and even if it is troublesome for a time it will gradually fade out.

Bless your body. If there is anything wrong with a particular organ, bless that organ. Bless your home. Bless your business. Bless your associates. Turn any seeming enemies into friends by blessing them. Bless the climate. Bless the town, and the state, and the country.

Bless a thing and it will bless you.

So shall my word be that goeth forth out of my mouth: it shall not return unto me void, but it shall accomplish that which I please, and it shall prosper in the thing whereto I sent it (Isaiah 55:11).

The subject of diet is one of the foremost topics of the present day in public interest. Newspapers and magazines teem with articles and book shops are filled with volumes unfolding the mysteries of proteins and vitamins. Experts are saying that you become the thing you eat. This is perfectly true, as far as it goes, but I am going to deal with the subject of dieting at a level infinitely more profound and far-reaching in its effects—mental dieting.

The food you furnish your mind determines the character of your life. The subjects that you allow your mind to dwell upon, make your surroundings what they are. *As thy days, so shall thy strength be* (Deuteronomy 33:25), which in modern language may be translated "as thy thoughts so shall thy life be."

Everything in your life today—the state of your body, the state of your fortune, the state of your home, the present condition of every phase of your life—is entirely conditioned by the habitual tone of your past thinking. And the condition of your life next week, and next year, will be conditioned by the thoughts and feelings that you entertain from now onward. In other words, you choose your life.

Thought is the real causative force in life, and there is no other. You cannot have one kind of mind and another kind of environment. You cannot change your environment while leaving your mind unchanged. This is the real key to life; if you change your mind your conditions must change too—your body must change, your activities must change; your home must change; the color-tone of your whole life must change.

And be not conformed to this world: but be ye transformed by the renewing of your mind . . . (Romans 12:2).

This may be called the Great Cosmic Law. The practical difficulty in applying it arises from the fact that our thoughts are so close to us that it is difficult, without a little practice, to stand back and look at them objectively. Yet that is just what you must learn to do. You must train yourself to choose the subject of your thinking at any given time, and also to choose the emotional tone.

If you are not determined to start in now and carefully select all day the kind of thoughts that you are going to think, you may as well give up all hope of shaping your life into the kind of thing that you want it to be. The way to start on a seven-day mental diet is to begin now.

361

To train yourself in the habit of thought selection will be difficult for the first few days, but it is the most interesting experiment that you could possibly make. You will be amazed at the things that you will learn about yourself. This week may be the most significant week in your whole life; not only will you be able to face your present difficulties in a better spirit, but the difficulties will go. You cannot change conditions directly—you have often tried to do so and failed—but go on the seven-day mental diet and conditions must change for you.

This then is your prescription. For seven days you must not allow yourself to dwell for a moment on any kind of negative thought. You must watch yourself for a week and must not under any pretense allow your mind to dwell on any thought that is not positive, constructive, optimistic, kind. This discipline will be so strenuous that you could not maintain it consciously for much more than a week, but a week will be enough, because by that time the habit of positive thinking will begin to be established. Some changes for the better will have come into your life, encouraging you enormously, and then the new way of life will be so attractive that you will find your mentality aligning itself almost automatically.

Watch and pray, that ye enter not into temptation: the spirit indeed is willing, but the flesh is weak (Matthew 26:41).

What is meant by negative thinking? A negative thought is any thought of failure, disappointment, or trouble; any thought of criticism, or spite, or jealousy, or condemnation of others, or self-condemnation; any thought of sickness or accident; or, in short, any kind of limitation. In practice you will never have any trouble in knowing whether a given thought is positive or negative. Even if your brain tries to deceive you, your heart will whisper the truth.

Second, you must be quite clear that what this scheme calls for is that you shall not dwell upon negative things. It is not the thoughts that come to you that matter, but only such of them as you choose to entertain and dwell upon. Many negative thoughts will come to you all day long. Some will be given to you by other people, or you will hear disagreeable news. These things, however, do not matter so long as you do not entertain them. An analogy is furnished by the case of a man who is sitting by an open fire when a red hot cinder flies out and falls on his sleeve. If he blows that cinder off at once, without a moment's delay to think about it, no harm is done. But if he allows it to rest on him for a single moment, under any pretense, the mischief is done, and it will be a troublesome task to repair that sleeve. So it is with a negative thought.

Repent therefore of this thy wickedness, and pray God, if perhaps the thought of thine heart may be forgiven thee (Acts 8:22).

People often find that the starting of this seven-day mental diet seems to stir up difficulties. It seems as though everything begins to go wrong at once. This may be disconcerting, but it is really a good sign. Suppose your whole world seems to rock on its foundations. Hold on steadily, let it rock, and when the rocking is over, the picture will have reassembled itself into something much nearer to your heart's desire.

Do not tell anyone else that you are on a diet. Remember that your soul should be the Secret Place of the Most High. When you have secured your new mentality, then tell the story to anyone else whom you think is likely to be helped by it.

Tell ye your children of it, and let your children tell their children, and their children another generation (Joel 1:3).

All the old traditions tell us that there is more than one path to the great Goal. Just as there is more than one road up every great mountain, and yet all roads meet at the top, so in the spiritual quest there are several roads, all of which lead in due season to the one great End.

There is the path of knowledge. True knowledge of divine things is one of the appointed paths to attainment; but that path is by no means for everyone. And there is the pathway of action—of organized activity—and the world needs this too; but this again usually calls for a special gift, and special circumstances in which to apply it. And there are others.

The shortest and the easiest pathway of all is the pathway of Love. It is the one pathway that is open to all, irrespective of what their personal conditions or circumstances may be. For everyman, everywhere, the true attainment awaits through the yoga of Love, for yoga means union and it is our union with God that makes the attainment possible.

There is no fear in love; but Perfect love casteth out fear: because fear hath torment . . . (1 John 4:18).

. . . *God is Love; and he that dwelleth in love dwelleth in God, and God in him* (1 John 4:16).

The way of Love, upon which you may step at any moment—at this moment if you like—requires no formal permit, has no entrance fee, and no conditions whatever. You need no expensive laboratory in which to train, because your own daily life, and your ordinary daily surroundings, are your laboratory. You need no reference library, no professional training; no external acts of any kind. All you need is to begin steadfastly to reject from your mentality everything that is contrary to the law of love.

You must build up by faithful daily exercise the true Love Consciousness. Love will heal you. Love will comfort you. Love will guide you. Love will illumine you. Love will redeem you from sin, sickness, and death, and lead you into your promised land.

Say to yourself: "My mind is made up; I have counted the cost; and I am resolved to attain the Goal by the path of Love. Others may pursue knowledge, or organize great enterprises for the benefit of humanity, or scale the austere heights of asceticism; but I have chosen the path of Love. My own heart is to be my workshop, my laboratory, my great enterprise, and love is to be my contribution to humanity."

And we know that all things work together for good to them that love God (Romans 8:28).

PRAYERS AND MEDITATIONS

My soul is filled with divine Love. I am surrounded by divine Love. I radiate Love and Peace to the whole world. God is Love, and all men are expressions of divine Love.

The Love of God burns in me for all humanity. I am a lamp of God, radiating divine Love to all whom I meet, to all whom I think of.

Jesus said: *A new commandment I give unto you, That ye love one another; as I have loved you. . . . By this shall all men know that ye are my disciples, if ye have love one to another* (John 13:34).

God is love; and he that dwelleth in love dwelleth in God, and God in him (1 John 4:16).

There is no fear in love; but perfect love casteth out fear: because fear hath torment. He that feareth is not made perfect in love (1 John 4:18).

Beloved, let us love one another: for love is of God; and every one that loveth is born of God, and knoweth God. He that loveth not knoweth not God; for God is love (1 John 4:7–8).

For this is the message that ye heard from the beginning, that we should love one another (1 John 3:11).

We love him, because he first loved us (1 John 4:19).

God is fully present here with me, now. God is the only real Presence—all the rest is but shadow. God is perfect Good, and God is the cause only of perfect Good. The same fountain cannot send forth both sweet and bitter water. God never sends sickness, trouble, accident, temptation, nor death itself; nor does He authorize these things.

I am divine Spirit. I am the child of God. In God I live and move and have my being; so I have no fear. I am surrounded by the Peace of God and all is well. I dwell in the Presence of God, and no fear can touch me. I am not afraid of the past; I am not afraid of the present; I am not afraid for the future; for God is with me. The eternal God is my dwelling place and underneath are the everlasting arms. Nothing can ever touch me but the direct action of God Himself, and God is Love.

While I live will I praise the Lord: I will sing praise unto my God while I have any being.

There is no power but of God. God is Love. God is the strength of my heart. God is my strength and power, and he maketh my way perfect. He guideth my way in perfectness.

When my soul fainted within me I remembered the Lord: and my prayer came unto thee. I will fear no evil: for thou art with me. Thou art my refuge and my fortress: my God; in thee will I trust. I will rejoice in thy salvation.

My Father and I are One. If I take the wings of the morning, and dwell in the uttermost parts of the sea, even there shall thy hand lead me, and thy right hand shall hold me.

The Bible says:

In the beginning was the Word, and the Word was with God, and the Word was God (John 1:1).

He sent his word, and healed them, and delivered them from their destructions (Psalm 107:20).

And they were astonished at his doctrine: for his word was with power (Luke 4:32).

So shall my word be that goeth forth out of my mouth: it shall not return unto me void, but it shall accomplish that which I please, and it shall prosper in the thing whereto I sent it (Isaiah 55:11).

For the word of God is quick, and powerful, and sharper than any two-edged sword (Hebrews 4:12).

❦

There is no difficulty that enough love will not conquer; no disease that enough love will not heal; no door that enough love will not open; no gulf that enough love will not bridge; no wall that enough love will not throw down; no sin that enough love will not redeem.

It makes no difference how deeply seated may be the trouble, how hopeless the outlook, how muddled the tangle, how great the mistake; a sufficient realization of love will dissolve it all.

God is Infinite Life. God is Boundless Love. God is Infinite Intelligence. God is Unfathomable Wisdom. God is Unspeakable Beauty. God is the Unchanging Principle of Perfect Good. God is the soul of man.

I am the image and likeness of God, and I have the power of His Word. His Word goes forth charged with His power.

Now I speak His Word in your name and in mine and I say that the full power of God is now awakened in you, filling your soul with peace and life and joy. Your Soul is as the burning bush that burned with the power of God and was not consumed. There are no dark corners left; no complexes or neuroses; no fears or doubts; no old dark things.

The peace of God surrounds you and fills you. That peace goes with you as a pillar of cloud by day and a pillar of fire by night.

God is now working to move you into your true place. One Presence, one Power, and one Mind. You are part of that divine Presence and in that Presence you dwell forever.

According to your faith be it unto you (Matthew 9:29).

I have the power to change my mentality and when I change it my outer expression and experiences must change too. I have the power to choose my thoughts; no one else can keep me from my true place.

All things are ready: I have knowledge, intelligence, all I need. I am a timeless being outside of time and space. I am going to live forever, as all men are, for I am one with God.

The false belief of limitation and fear that I have had no longer has any power over me. My body is joyous and free.

I am hemmed in by what seems a very real doubt of myself. But if I use my own true talents, the way will open out before me. I need not work to make this true. IT IS TRUE.

❦

God is Life. I understand that and express it. God is perfect Truth. I understand that and express it. God is Love. I understand that and express it. I radiate thoughts of love and peace and healing to the whole universe. If anyone has ever injured me or done me any harm, I fully and freely forgive him now, and the thing is done forever. I go free.

God is boundless Wisdom. That Wisdom is mine. That Wisdom leads and guides me; so I shall not make mistakes. The Christ in me is a lamp unto my feet. God is life substance, and that substance is my supply; so I cannot lack. The Lord is my Shepherd, I shall not want. God is mind, one infinite, divine, perfect mind. There is nothing to challenge the power of that mind, of that being. I have nothing to protect myself from but my own fear and doubt and selfishness.

❧

God is light, and in Him is no darkness at all. God is light, and love, and unspeakable beauty, and the beauty and glory of His presence now fills your soul. Your soul is a temple of the living God. It is filled with peace and harmony, and joy. There are no shadows left; no dark corners. Your soul is filled with the golden light of the presence of God Himself. All old fears, old regrets, old resentments melt away in the presence of God. You have forgiven everyone; you have set everyone free this morning, so now you are free yourself; so on this the morning of the Resurrection, you have partaken of the Resurrection.

I am energy. I am strength. I am power. I am filled with omnipotent life. The vitality of God permeates every fiber of my being. I am well and whole in every part of my body. The grace and poise of our Lord, Jesus Christ, enfolds me. I have nothing to deal with but my own thoughts. God has no difficulties to overcome. When God speaks the whole world is made fresh.

I claim God is the only Presence and the only Power. I have conscious realization of the Presence of God within me. I claim God is Infinite Life and that Life is my supply, so I shall want for nothing. God created me and God sustains me so all is well.

I claim that God will enlighten and teach me all the things I need to know. In some good way all the things I need to know will come to me.

I claim that God is Infinite Spirit, Perfect and Pure. I am divine Spirit, therefore I am Perfect and Pure. I am the image and likeness of God. In God I live and move and have my being.

I claim that God is unfathomable Wisdom and that Wisdom is mine. It leads and guides me so I shall not make mistakes, for God is the only door.

I claim a conscious realization of the Christ within me. The Christ within me is Perfect and Understanding.

I am the divine Spirit. In God I live, and move, and have my being. I am part of the self-expression of God, and I therefore express perfect harmony. I individualize Omniscience. I have direct knowledge of Truth. I have perfect intuition. I have spiritual perception. God is my Wisdom; so I cannot err. God is my Intelligence; so I am always thinking rightly. There is no waste of time, for God is the only Doer. My work is always well done, for my work is God's work.

The Holy Spirit is continually inspiring me. My thoughts are fresh, and new, and clear, and powerful with the might of Omnipotence. My prayers are the handiwork of the Holy Ghost— powerful as the eagle and gentle as the dove. They go forth in the name of God Himself, and they cannot return unto me void. They shall accomplish that which I please, and prosper in the thing whereto I send them. I thank God for this.

There is only one presence, God, and God is infinite Intelligence, and infinite Love, and has All Power. In truth and reality every person on earth is a spiritual being and expresses all these divine qualities. All men and women realize divine wisdom, and express it in their thoughts, and words, and deeds. The children of God have perfect understanding and seek only to do the will of God. So there is only one great plan and purpose—divine harmony. Only good, and truth, and divine love can be thought or expressed by anyone because God is the only Cause.

I am not trying to bring these things about—I could not—but with the eye of faith I perceive them to be true now, and I rejoice in this and thank God for it.

When you have made your prayer, forget the subject until the next day. On no account should you think about negative things while you are praying. Do not think of war or death or danger of any kind, for instance. Your prayer is a visit with God, and nothing evil can live in His presence.

He leadeth me in the paths of righteousness for his name's sake. Righteousness means right thinking, and I know that to think rightly about any condition means healing and safety. Christ in me, my Good Shepherd, is now guiding me in the path of Right Thought; so all will be well. The nature of God is all-powerful, omnipresent good, boundless love. I know that this Boundless Love is now taking care of me, and arranging all my affairs.

God knows me, and loves me, and cares for me. I am just as dear to Him as any human being who has ever lived.

God has every quality of personality except limitation. He can be to me anything that any human being could be, and infinitely more.

In Truth and reality nothing can ever touch me but the direct action of God Himself, and God is Love.

There is no problem bigger than God. No difficulty, however seemingly grave, can come into my life, that God cannot completely wipe out.

God is continually instructing me and inspiring me, and in some good way He will now clearly show me the next important step in my life—and how to take that step.

The Will of God for me is peace of mind, true place, happiness, joyous activity, and unbroken progress—I thank God for this.